QUICKB

&

ACCOUNTING

A Complete and Comprehensive Guide
to Bookkeeping and Accounting for
Beginners

By John Kent

Table of Contents

QUICKBOOKS

A Comprehensive Guide to Bookkeeping and Learning Techniques on QuickBooks Software for Beginners

By John Kent

INTRODUCTION

The world is changing rapidly, and a lot of people have now become entrepreneurs. Many people have started their own businesses or are planning to do so. Start-up culture has now reached the grassroots. Due to this, a lot of new business people and entrepreneurs have start-ups. People keep on coming up with new ideas and plans to earn money.

Although a lot of people start new businesses every day, not all of them succeed. There are a multitude of reasons behind this including lack of planning, lack of market research, lack of business sense, lack of understanding, etc. are some of the most prominent reasons why businesses tend to fail. Another very common reason why businesses tend to fail is that new and many times experienced business owners do not know how to handle their accounts or do not consider them important enough. This is a grave error that has cost a lot of people their successful enterprises. It is thus recommended to learn as much as possible about accounting and bookkeeping.

Nowadays, thanks to the evolution of technology, there are many online and computerized bookkeeping and accounting software packages available on the market. All of these have different and interesting features that have made them quite popular. But most of these software packages are either too costly or do not have a lot of essential tools. But one software is sure to stand out from the crowd - QuickBooks.

QuickBooks is a highly advanced accounting and bookkeeping software created by Intuit. It is an interesting combination of many different accounting related functions and features in one single shell that is extremely easy to use and user-friendly as well. It helps people to stop relying excessively on spreadsheets, multiple tables, and tracking sheets as well. It performs a lot of intricate tasks automatically. It maintains a lot of accounting as well as financial tasks on a daily basis for you, automatically. Many people find filing taxes a complex and complicated process. QuickBooks can help you simplify this process because it will quickly and easily reconcile accounting figures.

One of the best things about this software is that it is highly customizable, and users can change and customize it according to their needs and requirements. Many users use a highly customized version of the program that is suited to their firm or industry.

If you are a beginner to the world of QuickBooks and find it kind of confusing, complex, or even scary, then don't worry. This book will help you learn the basics and advanced information about QuickBooks that can help you become the master of QuickBooks. It will help you learn the basics that can be used to maintain your finances and record your business dealings as well. It should be noted that QuickBooks is not just a program that records your daily transactions and deals. It can also be used for various other purposes as well. For instance, it can help you keep track of your finances, keep track of your customers, and keep track of your receipts and payments as well. This program contains everything that a new and budding (or even an expert) businessman may need. This book will get you started in the world of QuickBooks. It will help you study QuickBooks in depth.

Let us begin this journey together, one chapter at a time! Good luck!

CHAPTER ONE

WHY USE QUICKBOOKS?

Self-Employed

Managing your accounts, along with understanding and following your taxes, can be an especially difficult task if you are a self-employed individual. It can prove to be nerve-wracking and time-consuming, even if you are an expert at these two things. For many, this happens because you can't divide your work with other people, and you are forced to do everything on your own. While being self-employed is a great way to achieve success while being your own boss, it can be quite problematic as well, especially when you are bombarded by tasks from all directions. But don't worry, QuickBooks can help you solve at least a couple of problems. That way, you will have ample free time to deal with others.

QuickBooks is a great bookkeeping software that can help you on the go!

QuickBooks is best suited for self-employed individuals as it is simple to use and is quite effective as well. The best thing about QuickBooks is that it is available in two versions - desktop and mobile. You create invoices, employee records, and various other key items using QuickBooks. Along with this, you can also reconcile bank accounts, record payments, and create details versions of loss and profit reports as well. All of this can be done using a single interface.

There are a variety of reasons why you, as a self-employed individual, should use QuickBooks Self-Employed. Let us have a look at them one by one.

It allows you to divide expenses between personal and business.

There are many business accounting software packages available on the market, but most of them only allow users to sync credit cards, bank accounts, and payment accounts. This way, many freelancers, who are generally self-employed, cannot divide their business expenses, which are often on the edge of personal and professional expenses. These expenses include Internet service, phones, texting services, etc. What makes QuickBooks special is that you can flag items as business or personal. You can also flag them as split.

While personal and business options are great, the split option is highly useful for self-employed people. It allows you to split the expenses on the basis of the percentage of the total transaction, or the dollar amount as well. It is also possible to set up split transactions that are generally used for personal or professional requirements. These expenses will be filtered automatically. This way, you will not miss any deductions.

Ease of Use

While all versions of QuickBooks are easy to use, the Self-Employed version makes it extremely easy to make rules on the basis of payments and purchases. It is quite simple to link your bank account to QuickBooks.

It is possible to review a list of transactions and then flag them as split, personal, or business. While flagging, you can also make rules for revenues and expenses simultaneously. These rules are generally created around vendor or client names. Thus, this method will perhaps be useless for people who get paid by personal cheques. For such transactions, you will have to choose the categories manually. While this method may not work for 'side-jobs,' it is great for ongoing revenues. This will make the whole process smooth and timesaving.

One of the best things about QuickBooks is that you do not need to use any form of coding to create rules. Rules can be created by simple menus and point and click operation. Thus, the learning curve for QuickBooks is extremely easy.

Tax Prediction

One of the biggest problems that freelancers generally face is how to calculate taxes. For a self-employed person calculating and managing taxes is not only frustrating but also a time-consuming task. But it is unavoidable as well. QuickBooks can help you save a lot of time by calculating and estimating taxes for you.

Whenever the user tags a transaction as a business transaction, QuickBooks automatically calculates and predicts the tax owned. This number is displayed all the time on the dynamic dashboard in the software. This can help you to save a lot of time and patience. You can use this saved time in any other important activity or your business. It also allows you to plan the payments and taxes efficiently.

The only problem with this method is that you cannot flag deposit transactions as business transactions if the taxes have been removed already. If you try to do this, the prediction will become messed up. In simple terms, if you label something as a business deposit, the mechanism will think that you have not paid any taxes.

This can be a problem for many self-employed people and freelancers where often the taxes are cut from the income and also at places where the taxes are deducted from the income already. But this does not mean that the function is totally useless - rather, it has many uses. You just need to find out how to utilize them for your own benefits while avoiding any misinformed decisions.

Impeccable Design

One of the best things about QuickBooks is the dashboard design. It is pretty and extremely well made. It does not look cheap or complicated. It is quite user-friendly and aesthetically pleasing as well. Its clean design is best for users who are not accustomed to the workings of bookkeeping software. It is easy to navigate and use. The main menu, which is present at the top left corner of the window allows you to access a variety of options, including Transactions, Home, Miles (used to record mileage), Reports, Taxes, and Invoices.

Another great innovation present on the dashboard is the snapshot option. In this option, all the menus present in the Main Menu are available as well. Along with the above options, there are also other options, including Loss, Profit, Accounts, Expenses, and Estimated Due Taxes.

Along with the above options, a to-do list is available as well. In this to-do list, there are multiple things, including recent transactions, additional tax information, etc.

Another great aspect about this software is that it can be easily synced with TurboTax. It also has a Tax Checklist, which is time-sensitive. This way, you will never have to wait for an accountant to put in your taxes until the last minute. This will make your life hassle-free.

Online Invoices and Payments

One of the most boring and tedious jobs regarding freelancing is tracking the progress of payment of different invoices. QuickBooks can help you avoid this problem efficiently. Using this software, you can issue invoices directly from the software itself. Similarly, you can also set and change due dates and process payments accordingly. If you do choose to make payments online, then you can also enable other options such as account transfers and credit card payments. It is also possible to use both of these options together. The receipts of these invoices will be directly sent to your email so that you can check them any time you want.

Whenever an invoice is not flagged as paid, and the due date for the invoice has passed, the software will automatically calculate it as an overdue invoice. This will be displayed on the dashboard and the main Invoice tab as well. You can choose to either resend the invoice, or you can also follow up with the client.

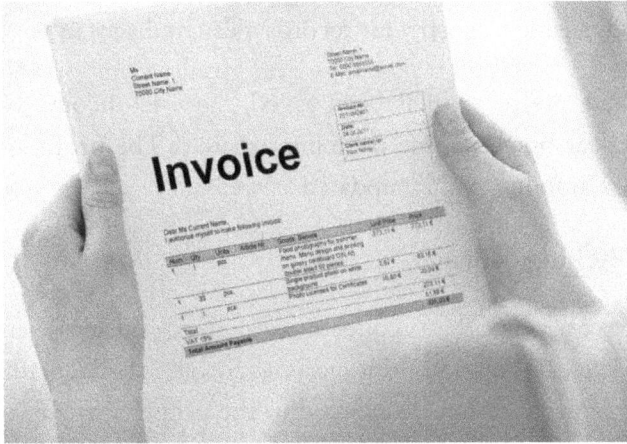

Managing Transactions in QuickBooks

QuickBooks Self-Employed is great and easy to use the cash-based system. In this system, you need to enter all the expenses and the payments that you receive, manually. This may sound like a difficult and time-consuming job, but it really is not. It is simple as adding transactions does not take more than a couple of seconds. It is also possible to add transactions by scanning or uploading receipts and invoices.

Adding transactions in this app is easy. You just need to click on the "Transactions" link present on the left of your window. Next, select "Add Transactions" on the top right. Next, select the type of transaction. This will mostly be business income or business expenses. Once this is done, you need to enter the total, description, and the category of the transaction. A long list of categories is available to keep your records clean and accessible.

Once the record has been saved, the total income will appear on the home page immediately. The profit and loss amounts will be updated as well.

Tracking Mileage

A very important concept related to business and finance is mileage. Mileage is a crucial, tax-deductible expense. It is rarely recorded in the proper way. If you fail to claim the proper transport expenses for your business, you will perhaps pay more tax than necessary. QuickBooks Self-Employed can help you in this case as it makes the whole process extremely easy.

You can enter your business trips with ease using the desktop version of the software, or you can also use the mobile app for the same task. The only thing that you need to do is to enter the proper start and end address. Your app will calculate the miles traveled automatically, and then based on your tax profile, will then calculate the deductible mileage expenses.

If you find this too time-consuming, you can also use the automatic mileage tracking option. This option is available in the mobile app. To use this, just start your mobile app when you are about to begin your journey. When you start your journey, just swipe and continue to drive. Stop the app once you reach your destination. The app will automatically calculate the number of miles of your travel and will show the same in your account. Thus, this method will not only save you a lot of time but will prevent a lot of unnecessary frustration as well.

QuickBooks and Taxation

Another great thing about QuickBooks is that it enables you to create your tax profile with ease. It features al the required information that is necessary for the calculation of your annual tax bill. For instance, in the United Kingdom, you need to enter your marital status and your personal tax-free allowance as well. The summary page will display all the necessary expenses and income. It will also show your tax liabilities at the end of the page. These are the only things that are generally required to file an online tax return.

Reporting

The report feature of the software is great as it not only provides you a simple tax summary, but it also has a list of all your current tax details. It is necessary to keep your tax data up to date and correct. If the information is not updated, the calculation of tax liabilities may go haywire.

You will also find the 'Profit and Loss' option in this section. The 'Profit and Loss' report is a complete analysis of your expenses, income, liabilities, assets, and profit. It is possible to view the reports of the current tax year and the previous tax year in many different options. For instance, you can view the reports by month, by year, or by quarters as well. The expenses are generally present at the bottom of the page, while your income and turnover are reported at the top. Your taxable profit is present under the 'Net Income' section.

Handling Invoices inside QuickBooks

QuickBooks Self-Employed has an in-depth invoice section that is great for keeping track of your payments and bills. You can keep track of the bills that have been paid and those that have not been paid. It is necessary to understand that the settled invoices are not carried forward to the tax summary and profit and loss report on its own. If you mark your invoice as 'Paid,' you will still have to create a transaction for the amount to avoid causing problems.

Creating an invoice in this software is easy. Just click on the 'Create invoice' option, which is present at the top of the screen. A box named 'Client name' will be visible. If the client is a new one, which means that you have never invoiced him or her before, then it is necessary to input his or her details. These details include full name, contact details such as phone number, and email address. If you plan to send the invoice to an old (or existing) client, then the details will be filled automatically.

Once the client has been added, you need to 'Add work.' In this box, you need to enter a few details regarding the nature of the job. A small description will suffice. You will be presented with an option to choose either an hourly rate or a flat rate. Next, enter a cash value and then finally press 'Add to invoice.' In the relevant box, add the preferred payment details and then click 'Send invoice,' which will be present at the bottom of your page. It is recommended to check the invoice once again before sending it. You can also save the invoice as a draft for future use.

Once you receive the payment of the invoice, go to the invoice page again and click "Mark paid." The color of the link will turn green from gray. This will indicate that you have successfully finished the transaction.

Self-employment is indeed great as it allows you to enjoy things at your own pace. But managing accounts can be a difficult task, which is why you should use QuickBooks to solve all your problems.

Being self-employed doesn't leave too much spare time for admin and accounts. But you can make things a lot easier for yourself by using a comprehensive accounting software package such as QuickBooks.

Thus, it is clear that QuickBooks is a great product for self-employed people and freelancers. It is affordable and cost-effective. It is great for people who want to take their business to the next level and become more successful. It is a great, all-in-one choice that will solve all your accounting problems. If you ever need more functions, you can always move on to the next version.

CHAPTER TWO

OPERATING QUICKBOOKS

QuickBooks is a simple, easy to use, a small business accounting program that can be used to manage expenses, costs, sales, and can be used to keep track of day-to-day transactions as well. It can be used to pay bills, invoice customers, file taxes, generate plans and reports, etc. There are various iterations available for QuickBooks, which have a variety of features according to the needs and requirements of business owners.

As there are a variety of QuickBooks options available, it can sometimes seem to be a bit daunting. It is recommended to understand it thoroughly before using it. You should test all the bells and whistles of the program. This way, you will understand how the basics of the program, and you will not find it difficult to use.

What Tasks do Small Businesses Use QuickBooks For?

Generally, small business owners prefer to use QuickBooks to check their invoices, keep an understanding of their cash flows, and pay their expenses. Some business owners also tend to utilize it to generate monthly and annual financial reports. It can also be used to prepare annual and quarterly business taxes as well. Many people generally use QuickBooks themselves, but some small business owners also prefer to use in-house bookkeepers as well.

Manage Sales and Income

You can check your income and sales using QuickBooks. This can be done by creating new invoices to track customer sales. It is recommended to use this function to keep in mind what your customers owe to you. This can be done if you know how to review your Accounts Receivable Aging Report. In this report, you can find the details about your current as well as old due invoices.

Check Expenses and Bills

QuickBooks can also be used to keep track of your bills along with expenses by connecting them directly to your bank, as well as a credit card account. This way, QuickBooks can keep track of your expenses by downloading them automatically and categorizing them as well. You can track cash transactions as well as check and record them in the QuickBooks in no time.

QuickBooks can also help you to pay bills before the due date. For instance, you can create an Accounts Payable Report, which will ensure that all your bills get paid on time. This report is great as it will allow having a look at all your current as well as past bills. This is great for troubleshooting if a problem arises in the future.

Reporting Insights

You can use QuickBooks to manage your cash inflow as well as outflow activities with ease. Due to this option, you can gain important insight related to your business efficiently. The reports are pre-built in QuickBooks. These reports can be accessed in a few simple clicks. These reports are updated automatically in real-time whenever you enter or save transactions.

This is especially great if you need to display your financials to a would-be investor or if you want to show them to your lender.

Along with the above-mentioned Accounts Receivable Report as well as the Accounts Payable Report, you can also have the following three reports to understand the health of your business. These reports are:

- Profit and Loss Report

- Balance Sheet Report

- Statement of Cash Flows

Let us have a look at these three reports one by one:

Profit and Loss Report

The profit and loss report can be created quickly. In this report, you can check how profitable you are as it contains a summary of your income from which your expenses are subtracted. It thus displays your bottom-line net income for a stipulated period; a week, a month, or even a quarter

Balance Sheet Report

The second report that can be used to study the health of your business is the Balance Sheet Report. In this report, you can check Liabilities, Assets, and Equity for your business at any specific point. You can create a balance sheet report in no time.

Statement of Cash Flow

The third report that you can create to check the health of your business is the Statement of Cash Flow. In this report, you can check the activities that affect your financing, investing, and operations of cash inflow as well as cash outflow.

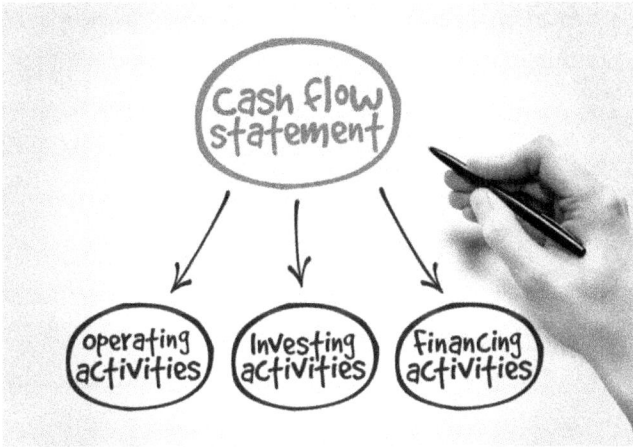

Run Payroll

Payroll is a crucial aspect of any financial firm. You should avoid making any errors or mistakes in this section. If you make any mistakes while calculating a paycheck, it can lead to a lot of problems, including unhappy employees and high penalties as well. To solve this, QuickBooks has its own payroll option, which can calculate and run payroll automatically whenever you need it.

The QuickBooks payroll option is integrated with QuickBooks; this way, all your financial statements remain up to date all the time. It is recommended to buy

QuickBooks payroll subscription so that you can utilize the payroll functions with ease.

Here is a small list of all the pros of using the payroll functions of QuickBooks:

- It can calculate the state as well as federal payroll taxes automatically

- You can pay employees with direct deposits or checks as well

- The program fills your tax forms automatically

- You can e-pay using QuickBooks

Track Inventory

You can use QuickBooks to keep track of your inventory as well. You can input details such as unit costs and on-hand amounts. QuickBooks will automatically track and update the details for you according to the transactions. In QuickBooks, there is a multitude of options that can be used to manage the inventory.

Tracking your inventory in an Excel sheet can take a lot of time and effort. But you can save these efforts and time by using QuickBooks.

Simplification of Taxes

QuickBooks can help you simplify your taxes significantly. You do not need to put a lot of time and effort into this. Taxes take a lot of time. It does not matter if you have all the receipts or if you have been tracking them meticulously in a spreadsheet file, ultimately, it will take you a lot of effort to file your tax returns.

QuickBooks can simplify this process a great deal. You can manage your business accounts and taxes using QuickBooks. You just need to set up your tax professional and allow him or her to access your QuickBooks data to collect information that is required to file tax returns. QuickBooks tracks everything meticulously, which is why you do not need to waste time organizing bank statements and receipts. This makes the whole process accurate, timesaving, and effortless as well.

Accept Online Payments

To make cash flow quick, efficient, and user-friendly, you should allow your customers to pay your invoices online. This can be quite difficult to manage, but you can do it with ease using QuickBooks. It is possible to add the Intuit Payments feature to your QuickBooks to enable online payment options with just a simple click of a button.

Once this option is activated, you can send invoices using email. All your emails will now have a "Pay Now" button as well. Whenever you send an invoice to a customer, he or she will be able to click the button and pay the invoice using their bank account or using any major credit cards they may have. This makes transactions hassle-free.

You do not need to pay any sort of monthly fee to use this option. You just need to pay the following charges:

- Bank Transfers (ACH) – Free

- Card Invoiced – 2.9% plus 25 cents

- Card Swiped – 2.4% plus 25 cents

- Card Keyed-in – 3.4% plus 25 cents

Scan Receipts

QuickBooks also allows you to scan your receipts, which makes the tax procedures effortless. If you are using QuickBooks Online, you can download the QuickBooks app on your mobile phones for free. Once you have downloaded the app, you can take pictures of the receipts and upload them to QuickBooks Online in no time.

Scanning the receipts and uploading them to QuickBooks Online will make your life stress-free. You will no longer have to worry about keeping and manually matching receipts. Similarly, you will never lose receipts anymore. You can upload any number of receipts to QuickBooks Online. This option is especially great for businesses that need to keep track of a lot of expenses, including law firms, lawyers, doctors, etc.

QuickBooks Features & Pricing

As said above, there are many different versions of QuickBooks available on the market. All of them have a variety of functions and options. These options change according to the need and requirements of the users. Before buying a QuickBooks version, it is recommended to have a look at different options and check that suits your needs the most. Let us have a look at the options in brief.

QuickBooks Online

This is one of the most used versions of QuickBooks as it does not require any kind of software installation, and it can be used from anywhere, as all the data is stored in the cloud. This version is available in three different versions, which are Simple, Essential, and Plus. It is highly recommended for all service-based firms and businesses that do not use complicated invoices. You can access the data stored on QuickBooks Online from any computer if you have the login details and an Internet connection.

QuickBooks Desktop

Like QuickBooks Online, QuickBooks Desktop comes in three different versions. These are Pro, Premier, and Enterprise. Unlike QuickBooks Online, you need to install software on your computer to use this version. This version is great for small businesses that are not into manufacturing. It is great for retailers, non-profit businesses, contractors, etc. The Enterprise version of the QuickBooks Desktop, as the name suggests, is best for large enterprises. This version is often considered to be industry-specific as it features reports and custom chart of accounts for the company.

QuickBooks Self-Employed

Nowadays the number of people who are either self-employed or are freelancers has increased significantly. QuickBooks has an option for such people as well. QuickBooks Self-Employed is a great product for freelancers, contractors, self-employed people, Lyft or Uber drivers, and real estate agents. It is based on the cloud-like QuickBooks Online. You can access this version from any computer if you have the login details and an Internet connection. The best thing about this version is that it has a multitude of features that are not present in any other version of QuickBooks. These features include the option to keep personal and business expenses separate, to transfer data to TurboTax, and to track miles as well.

It can also calculate and estimate your tax payments and can also remind you whenever they are due.

QuickBooks Mac

QuickBooks Mac, as the name suggests, is the only desktop version available for Mac users. If you do not want to use QuickBooks Online, then you can use this version if you have a Mac computer. This product is quite similar to the QuickBooks Pro. It is suitable for small businesses and firms that are not into manufacturing.

CHAPTER THREE

PAYROLL

Payroll is essential for business owners if you want to save money, pay your employees properly, and manage your taxes. Setting up and running payroll is extremely easy if you use QuickBooks Online. In this chapter, let us have a look at the data that is required to set up a payroll. Then, let us have a look at the steps involved to run a payroll.

Adding the Intuit Payroll to your already present QuickBooks account can help your business grow exponentially. You will be able to reap a multitude of benefits such as same-day deposits, taxes, help in setting up payroll, etc. This makes it a great investment for any business.

Payroll Setup: Data that you need

Before running payroll in QuickBooks, you need to set it up in the QuickBooks Online version. This is a simple process that does not take a lot of effort or time. Before moving on to the step-by-step instructions regarding payroll set up, it is necessary to have a look at some documents that are absolutely necessary for setting it up. Here is a list of all the documents that you need to set up a payroll.

Add Employer Information

Before setting up your payroll account, you need to have a business bank account and the routing number of the account. This account will be used to make tax payments and to pay the employees as well. Along with this, you need to have the salary information or the hourly rate of the employees as well. You should also be aware of other perks, including health insurance, retirement plans, incentives, etc. Here is a list of things that you must have:

Bank Account Information

You must have the account number and the routing number of the checking account from which you are going to write a check for the employees. This account is also used for making tax payments. (It is recommended to have a payroll account that will be different from your checking account that will be used for your daily business.

Employee Compensation

Under this section, you need to add the salaries, the hourly rates, tips, commissions, bonuses, and anything else that you give to your employees.

Employee Benefits

In this section, add any benefits that you provide to your employees. These include 401, dental insurance, health insurance, vacation policies, retirement policies, sick leave policy, and FSA or Flexible Spending Account.

Other

In this section, include anything else that is relevant. This section generally includes mileage reimbursement, cash advances, wage garnishments, union dues, etc.

Add Employee Info

QuickBooks cannot calculate payroll checks efficiently if you do not feed employee data in it. You need to have a variety of data, including Form W-4, deductions, pay rate, frequency of pay, etc.

Here is a small list of data that you need to enter in QuickBooks to successfully run a payroll:

Form W-4

When a firm or business hires a new employee, the employee needs to fill a form called Form W-4. In this form, the employee needs to add all withholding data along with any other important and pertinent information that is required to calculate the payroll tax deductions.

Pay Rate

This is the hourly rate or the salary that you pay employees. This section should also include any commission or bonus that you pay to employees (if applicable).

Paycheck Deductions

In this section, you need to add the employees' role in their retirement plans, health insurance, dental insurance, and garnishments.

Pay Schedule

In this section, you need to add the pay schedule of the employees. Generally, it is supposed to be weekly, twice a week, twice a month, or monthly. QuickBooks also offers you a flexible payment schedule. For instance, you also pay hourly employees every week, while salaried employees once a month, etc. Both of these pay schedules can be set up simultaneously.

Vacation or Sick Hours Policy

Generally, firms offer vacation or sick pay. For this, you need to input the information of all the employees. Generally, these hours are gained at the end of each pay period.

Hire Date

In this section, you need to enter the hiring date for each employee carefully.

Direct Deposit Authorization Form

In this section, you need to offer your employees the option of direct deposit as an alternative to check. To do this, you need to file the direct deposit authorization form. This will provide you with permission to make deposits into your employees' accounts. It will also allow you to rout the data required to make such deposits.

Doing payroll in QuickBooks is easy. In this section, let us have a look at the steps required to set up payroll in QuickBooks.

How to Set Up QuickBooks Payroll

In this section, let us have a look at the QuickBooks enhanced payroll service. Here is a list of steps that you need to undertake to run a payroll in QuickBooks Online successfully.

Go to the Employee Center

To begin the payroll process, you need to first click on the Employees tab, which is present on the left menu bar. A new window will open.

Payroll Setup

If you have bought the payroll service with QuickBooks Online subscription, then a window will appear on your screen. In this window, click on the "Get Set Up" button. A new window will appear. If you have not subscribed for payroll option yet, then you need to click on "Add Payroll." Once you have added payroll, you can click on the "Get Set Up" button.

Respond to the Questions

In the next window, you need to add some information. This is essential because you need to provide additional information to make the process smooth. This information is also required to make your W-2 forms accurate. To do this, you need to provide data related to any payrolls that you have issued during the year.

Add Employees

Once the above step is done, you can start adding employees to the program. To do so, just click on "Add an Employee." A new window will appear.

Complete Employee Info

In this step, you need to add the relevant and important information related to employees one by one.

Here is a list of all the fields that you need to fill in to run payroll successfully:

Employee Withholding Information

This data can be generally found in the Form W-4. To edit this section, just click on the Pencil icon.

Pay Schedule

To add this, just click on the 'Pay Schedule' option from the drop-down menu. There are a variety of options available in this section, including weekly, monthly, bimonthly, etc.

Employee Pay

As the name suggests, you need to enter the wages of the employees in this section. You can add different kinds of payment types in this section. To do so, just click on the 'Add Additional Pay Types' link, which is present under this field.

Employee Contribution/Deduction

In this section, you need to add the contributions or the deductions for the employees.

Payment Method

In this section, you need to select the mode of payment from the drop-down menu. Here you need to select from live check or direct deposit. If you choose direct deposit, then you need to input the bank details of the employee.

Year to Date Payroll

In this section, you need to enter last year's payroll information of the employee.

Finishing all these fields is essential, as it will reflect on your payroll system. It is required to fill the pertinent information of all the employees carefully. It is also recommended to double-check the data to avoid any mistakes. If you commit any errors here, your payroll calculations will turn out wrong as well.

How to Run Payroll in QuickBooks Online

In the last section, we saw how to set up your employees. In this section, let us have a look at how to run your payroll. In this section, you will learn how to input your payroll hours and other data using which your program will calculate the payroll checks and the payroll taxes automatically. You can then either print and pay the checks, or you can deposit them directly to the employees.

Let us have a look at the steps required to run payroll in QuickBooks Online.

Go to the Employee Center

Once again, go to the Employees tab situated on the left menu bar. A new window will open.

Click "Run Payroll"

In the new dashboard, you will see a list of employees that you set up using the steps given in the last section. Check the list and then click on the 'Run payroll' button situated in the top right corner.

Enter Current Payroll Hours

In the next screen, enter the total hours worked for hourly employees. Double-check other information. To enter hours as well as rates in the payrolls option, you need to fill in the following fields:

Bank Account

In this, you need to enter the details of the bank account from which the taxes and payroll checks are going to be deducted. If the bank details are incorrect, then change them from the drop-down menu.

Pay Period

In this section, you need to check the pay periods that you have entered in the last tutorial. If they are not correct, rectify them using the drop-down menu.

Pay Date

In this section, you need to check the date of payment for your employees.

Hours Worked

In this section, you need to enter the hours for which the employees have worked. (Only in the case of hourly employees.)

Salary Employees

Here, the program will calculate the annual salary automatically. Just crosscheck it once to ensure that it is correct.

Total Pay

In this section, the gross total of the pays of all the employees present on payroll will be given.

Review & Submit Payroll

In this step, you are supposed to check and review the data once again before finalizing it. If you believe that everything is accurate, you can move on; if not, go back and rectify the errors. Once you are satisfied with the details, click on the Submit button at the bottom of the page. Use the on-screen directions to either print the checks or the print the direct deposit slips.

Congratulations! You have successfully run your first payroll using QuickBooks.

CHAPTER FOUR

TRACKING RECEIPTS

Businesses and enterprises do not work on goodwill. You need to be meticulous and disciplined when running a business. If you are not disciplined or are too careless, you will never earn profit from your business. It is necessary to keep track of all the receipts that are collected while doing business. In this chapter, let us have a close look at receipts and how they are tracked.

Sales receipts are essential if you want to conduct your business successfully. Normally, if you work in retail, sales receipts are a must. You cannot function without sales receipts. It is necessary to pay close attention to sales receipts when you run an enterprise. It is required to take them seriously. These receipts contain crucial data, and they reflect the methods of your business accounting. Sometimes managing and creating these receipts can be a difficult and time-consuming task, but you can do it with ease using QuickBooks.

What Is a Sales Receipt?

Before moving on to the role of QuickBooks in the management of sales receipts, it is necessary to understand what sales receipts are. In simple terms, sales receipts are documents that show a sale. This document is essential as it acknowledges that the seller has paid for either services or goods. The receipt is given to the buyer by the seller.

Receipts are only provided once the service or the goods have been given to the customer. Generally, the customer needs to pay for these goods or services in full. In some cases, some businesses also issue partial receipts. This generally happens when a customer buys a costly or high-priced product and pays for it with the help of installments. Partial receipts are also issued when the seller offers a king of continuous service to the customer, and the customer pays the seller on a recurring basis as well. In such cases, the sales receipt generally shows the remaining balance as well.

What Information should be present on a Sales Receipt?

A variety of receipts are available in the world of finance. Generally, a seller designs the receipt according to his or her business. He or she can add anything he or she wants on the receipt, but there are certain things that need to be on the receipt, or it becomes useless. Here is a small list of items that should be present on the receipt:

- The name of the product or service

- The UPC of the service or the product

- The quantity of the service or the product

- The sale price of the service or the product

- The total amount of the sale

- The rate of sales tax

- The amount of tax

- The total price of the tax

In the case of tax, it is necessary to create correct and complete receipts. If the receipts are inaccurate, then the tax calculation will be erroneous.

To make a receipt more useful, it is recommended to add the following details on your receipt.

- The GST registration number of the seller

- The date, address, and time of the sale

- The name of the business

- The contact information of the business. This includes email address, phone number, or website.

- The name of the sales associate who did the business

- Along with these, you can also add the following items to your receipt:

- Customer information including name and contact number

- Company logo

- Branding material

- Coupons

- Marketing copy

What are Gift Receipts?

Almost all receipts carry a standard amount of data, but there are certain receipts like gift receipts that are different from regular receipts. Gift receipts contain some pertinent information regarding the sale, but they generally do not contain the price of the product or service. This way, the recipient can give or take the product or the service without seeing the price. Certain gift receipts include the name of the products, but most of them only have a barcode that can be scanned by business people only. This is used to access the sales record of the particular product.

It solely depends on the seller whether the gift receipt will be held valid for returns or not. Generally, it is only valid for exchanges. Certain customers tend to ask for custom gift receipts as well. It is recommended to clarify the return and exchange policies to such customers to avoid any further nuisance.

The Importance of Receipts

Receipts are extremely crucial as they are the official sales records for your firm. It is necessary to safeguard them and manage them carefully. It is also necessary to create them correctly. Inaccurate receipts can lead to a lot of problems internally as well as externally. Internally, the receipts are used to track your sales and the amounts that you gain. This means that they can be used to calculate the cash flow, the profit statement, and the loss statement as well. This information is essential as it allows you to make proper and better business decisions.

It can also help you to make and understand long-term plans.

Externally, receipts are important because they are used for tax filing. As a business, it is your duty to record your sales as well as the tax that you charge your buyers. This information is crucial as it helps you to file and pay taxes properly. Without this information, you will not be able to pay taxes correctly. Sometimes you need to create a paper trail that can help you to prove your tax number and sales int eh case of an audit.

Detailed receipts are also important and useful for your buyers as well. They can help them to prove deductible expenses, record paid taxes, and track business costs as well. Thus, when they file taxes, the receipts can help them a lot.

What's the Difference between an Invoice and a Sales Receipt?

Invoices and sales receipts often seem to be similar, which is why people often confuse them. It is true that both of them are used to record sales and contain almost the same information. But they are still different. The differences lie in how they are used in accounting and how they are issued.

Generally, a receipt is the record of a sale that has been completed. It is normally issued after payment. For instance, if a customer bought B number of products at C price, got the products, and paid the total C price, then the customer will get a receipt. This is because the seller will have the money in his or her hand, and there will no further exchange or transaction of any sort. This sale will be written as income in your books. You can further deposit this amount in your bank. Unless the customer comes back for a return or refund, the sale is finished.

Invoices generally record an unfinished or partial transaction. They are generally issued before the payment is made. They are used to track the sale. Invoices are usually used in the service industry more than in the retail industry. For instance, when a homeowner signs a painter to paint his or her house, both parties agree on a price. The painter will then issue an invoice to the homeowner containing details such as records of the services that are to be done, the price of the service, and the date when it will be completed. Once the service gets done, the homeowner will clear the invoice and will get a receipt from the painter, who will denote that the transaction is done. Invoices are also used in the case of electricity bills, phone bills, and credit card statements as well.

Sometimes retail stores to issue invoices to buyers. Invoices are generally issued to customers who have credit accounts — this way, the customer can receive the product first and pay the price later.

As said above, invoices are recorded in a different way as compared to regular sales receipts. Companies generally consider invoices as receivables and not as income. This way, they understand that the sale is not complete and that it will be complete in the future. The sale or the amount can only be recorded as 'income' when the sale is complete and when the amount is deposited in the bank account.

Different Receipt Types for Different Industries

There exists no typical or standard format of receipt. Different companies and industries have different forms of receipts. But sometimes, certain forms become standard, unofficially. Here is a small list of different kinds of sales receipts that are generally used around the world. It needs to be understood that these are not hard and fast forms, and they change according to the industry and the needs and requirements of the seller.

Register Tape

This is a common form of receipt that is generally used in transactions where the customer comes face to face with the seller. The receipt is printed automatically and can be torn off instantaneously. It is great for companies that deal with high volume sales. These receipts are generally used in grocery stores, gas stations, and specialty shops as well.

Handwritten Carbons

This is another form of receipt that is often used in impromptu sales as well as the personal-service industry. For instance, landlords often use this method to acknowledge rent payment. These receipts are also used by businessmen who conduct their business out of temporary stalls or makeshift locations. These stalls are generally present at conventions, trade shows, etc.

Contractors who try to find new business in their respective fields such as roofing contractors, gardeners, landscapers, etc. who are supposed to visit the houses of customers generally use these receipts as well.

At the end of the week, you can collect and input the data collected from these receipts in your accounting system. Handwritten receipts are accepted in many states if they do not appear suspicious.

Invoices

These are extremely common in business-to-business records. Many buyers tend to ask for invoices in a specific manner for their own bookkeeping purposes. Invoices are generally printed and mailed or handed over, but nowadays, a lot of people send them online as well. Certain online payment processors can create an invoice according to the request of the payment. QuickBooks Online is better than such options as it allows you to create custom invoices according to the requirement of the customer. You can also set up a general format that can be used for all the other customers.

Packing Slips

These receipts are generally used by enterprises that deal with shipping. Such companies only ship the items to the customers and do not sell them in person. The packing slips contain a complete detailed list of all the items that have been shipped to you along with the prices of the items and the contact details of the company. Certain companies also include return labels as well. This slip is generally present in your delivery.

As said above, there are a variety of sales receipts that change according to the needs and requirements of the sellers, and in some cases, the customers as well.

How to Make a Sales Receipt

A variety of options are available to make your own small business receipts. These options depend on your needs, your requirements, the nature of your business, the level of personalization, the details that you want to use, and affordability. Your sales receipts and the information present on your receipts communicate your ideas to customers. Good receipts can help you bring in future customers who will feel comfortable dealing with you.

Generally, companies that use field sales associates tend to use handwritten receipts. These receipts are convenient options for such companies. While it is true that these receipts take a lot of time to be filled, they offer a lot of flexibility as well. This is because they are blank canvases in which you can input the data according to your requirements.

If you decide to use handwritten sales receipts, it is recommended to find pre-printed templates that will be suitable for your industry or business. For instance, if you have a landscaping business, it is recommended to find a blank template where details such as yard size, grass type, plants, etc. are mentioned. It should also have some details related to edging, fences, weeding, etc. Similarly, if you own a marketing business, your blank template should have details such as the number of hours, description of the service, the hourly rate, etc. If you are a new business, it is recommended to use handwritten receipts as they are not only easy to use, but they also offer you ample opportunity to refine and grow your business. Most handwritten receipts generally need only a receipt pad and pen. This makes them extremely cost-effective and efficient. It is recommended to make some stamps to make writing receipts effortless.

If you are a new company and you need occasional receipts, then you can make receipts on simple word processors such as LibreOffice or Microsoft Word as well. Most of these programs generally have inbuilt receipt templates that can be edited and customized according to the needs, requirements, and nature of your business. If you cannot find a decent receipt template, you can download a new one at affordable rates.

You can also design your own template from scratch. This option is best for users who like to have personalized and highly customized receipts. It is recommended to use tables in your receipt to make it easy to read and track. Tables will also help you to keep everything organized. It is recommended to highlight important details such as the name of the customer, the tax, the total, the grand total, the subtotal, etc. This option allows you to add anything you want to your receipt, including add-on services, ID numbers, details, etc.

Word Processors are also great if you run a shipping business. If you do not retail a lot of products, you can create manual receipts in word processors. If you make a lot of deals every day, then you can also link your sales database to the document. This way, the document will take all the relevant data automatically and save you a lot of time and effort. You can then print these receipts and put them in the shipment. It is easy to create PDFs using word processors, which makes emailing receipts a piece of cake.

While these methods are great if you have a small business where you have a lot of time to manage things, these methods can be quite time consuming if you have a large business. In the case of large businesses, it is recommended to use some dedicated receipt software, such as QuickBooks.

Creating Sales Receipts in QuickBooks Online

QuickBooks is a great program that can help you to create and email sales receipts from a desktop computer efficiently. If you have the QuickBooks Online version, then you can create and send sales receipts from any device that is connected to the Internet. So if your employees are on the field and want to create invoices on their tablets or phones, they can do so with ease. This intuitive and easy to use feature helps you to customize receipts according to the nature of your company. You can personalize your receipts according to your requirements.

It is extremely simple to create receipts in QuickBooks. It is also timesaving and takes merely a few moments to do so. When you open and sign in to QuickBooks account, just click the plus sign. Next, click on the Customers menu. Here, click on the Choose Sales Receipt, and a blank window will be presented on the screen. In the blank form, you input the necessary details that are pertinent to the sales receipt. This normally includes business name, customer's name, contact details, etc. If the customer is new, you can also save him or her as a frequent customer to avoid entering these details every time.

Once you have entered the name or the customer, add the items or the service that you sold. If you have a set of items that you sell, you can save these items in the inventory list so that you do not have to add the items every time you make a sales receipt. If you sell miscellaneous items, then avoid making inventories. Try to find other timesaving options and methods that will work for you.

Adding new items in QuickBooks is quick and easy. You can add a variety of details such as the name of the product, information related to the product, the ID number, or the description of the product as well. Once these details have been added, add the per-unit price for the product. You do not need to add the subtotal, as the program will calculate it with the help of prices and quantities of your products. QuickBooks knows your industry and location. This is essential because it can add the sales tax (if necessary) to the receipt automatically. If you ever want to change an item, remove it, or add it, or change the price of the item or update the quantity of the products, the total of the receipt will change as well.

Another feature that makes QuickBooks really efficient is that you can add discounts and tips using the program.

Once the receipt becomes ready, you get a variety of options. You can preview the final version of the receipt using the Print Preview option. If you find any problems or errors, you can make changes immediately. Once you are satisfied with the receipt, you can then save it to the database. You can then either print the receipt or send it to the customer directly.

One of the best things about receipt generators like QuickBooks is that it can be integrated into the accounts system with ease. This way, your bookkeeping functions become easy and coherent. Whenever you make a receipt, you can flag it as an income account or as an account receivable. The funds will then automatically get transferred to your financial records. You will not have to input them in a separate manner.

If your company generally does a lot of repeat deals with different people, QuickBooks can help you save a lot of time and energy. Once you input the information of a customer in QuickBooks Online, the information gets saved on the cloud. Next time whenever you want to create a receipt, you can use the auto-fill option to fill the information in the receipt. Even if you do not make repeated deals with a customer, the saved information can still be useful. You can access the saved information any time and check the details of the transaction quickly. The best thing about storing information and sales record online is that it is almost impossible to lose the data. It is always safe and secure. It is easy to lose hard copies of sales receipts. But virtual sales receipts rarely get lost. These sales receipts also have time stamps. This way, you can create a virtual 'paper' trail that cannot be changed. This paper trail is great for tax purposes. This method is also great for your customers who can check the expenses whenever they want. Thus, this method is great for both the sellers as well as customers.

Managing Sales Receipts for Your Small Business

Sales receipts are essential if you are a small business owner. These receipts can be used to keep a record of your finances accurately. But to manage these receipts, it is necessary to have a good receipt management system as well. For instance, you must have seen some restaurants with metal spikes near registers where receipts are pierced and stacked. This method is great for keeping the receipts safe until the end of the day. At the end of the day, the receipts are removed and then added to the books. Many people also tend to use special receipt drawers and receipt boxes as well.

If you want to use a modern method to save your records, you can save the digital copies as well. This can be done by maintaining the copies of the transactions on the server of the devices present at the point of sale. You can then use this data to fill your spreadsheet to maintain your books. If you enable autofill, then this data will be filled automatically. It is quite similar to the metal spike method, but it is more time-efficient and does not need a lot of papers as well. Thus, it is environment-friendly as well.

But there are many other options to manage your receipts, especially if you do not want to wait until the end of the day to manage your books. For instance, QuickBooks and similar programs can help you save the data in real-time on the cloud. Due to this, you can check data and total after each sale. Cloud-based programs are great because they can also allow you to print register tape while the employees are still working. Even if your employees are out in the field and are working, you can print out sales projections with ease. Just allow your employees to add data in the program, and the program will do the necessary work for you immediately.

CHAPTER FIVE

INVENTORY

Tracking and keeping a record of your inventory can be a difficult job, but you need to do it correctly to avoid any problems in the future. There are many methods of tracking and managing your inventory. While managing your inventory by hand is a decent option if you do not have a lot of items for sale if you have a lot of items, then managing an inventory manually can be quite difficult.

There are a variety of QuickBooks options available for your perusal. You can use inventory options in QuickBooks Pro, QuickBooks Premier, and QuickBooks Enterprise edition as well. These features are generally disabled when you install these programs. You can enable the functions and can begin with tracking in no time. Once these functions are activated, you can manage inventory with ease. You will also get alerts whenever you need to reorder items or whenever you need to purchase new products. Using the

QuickBooks inventory function is fairly easy, and you can start adding products to the inventory almost instantly.

Check Your Subscription First

Before beginning your inventory process, you need to check whether you are subscribed to the inventory option or not. If you are not subscribed to the function, then you will not be able to add entries in your inventory. Inventory management is not available with all the plans, so check whether you are subscribed to the inventory manager or not. To do this, open QuickBooks and click on the gear-shaped icon. This will open a menu. In this menu, select Accounts and Settings, and here click on Locate. Next, select the Billing and Subscription option. Here you can check your current plan. If you see that you are not subscribed to the Inventory function, then it is recommended to subscribe to it immediately to unlock the inventory-related features and functions in QuickBooks.

How to Set Up Inventory Parts and Non-Inventory Parts in QuickBooks

Once you confirm that you have subscribed to the inventory options in QuickBooks, it is time to add to the inventory.

It is possible to add both inventory and non-inventory items in the program. This is done for the reason of tracking. Inventory items are the items that are currently in stock. For instance, if you have a grocery business, then the number of certain cookies will be added to the inventory. Non-inventory items are the items that are not in stock but can be ordered specially on the request of customers.

To add inventory items to QuickBooks, you need to switch on the inventory tracking option. To add non-inventory parts, you do not need to change any settings. Let us now have a simple look at how to add items to inventory and non-inventory.

Inventory Parts

1. Open the QuickBooks program and click on 'Edit' from the menu bar.

2. In the Edit menu, choose 'Preferences.'

3. In this menu, click on 'Items and Inventory.'

4. Next, click on the 'Company Preferences' tab.

5. Check the box near 'Inventory and Purchase orders are active.' This will allow inventory tracking.

6. Click OK.

7. Click on 'Items and Services' in the Home window.

8. Click on the 'Item' button and then click on 'New.'

9. Click on 'Inventory Part' from the drop-down menu.

10. Input the name of the item in the 'Item Name/Number' box.

11. Click on the 'Income Account' drop-down menu. In this menu, choose the account that you would like to use to track the income of this inventory.

12. Add the remaining information and finally click 'OK.'

This will successfully create an inventory item.

Non-Inventory Parts

Adding non-inventory parts is easier than adding inventory parts. Let us have a look at the steps required to add non-inventory parts.

1. Click on the 'Items and Services' option in the Home window.

2. Click on the 'Item' button.

3. Click on the 'New' option to open a new item window.

4. Click on 'Non-inventory Part' from the drop-down menu.

5. Input the name of the item in the 'Item Name/Number' box.

6. Choose the account that you would like to link to the item using the drop-down menu.

7. Add any remaining and pertinent information and click 'OK.'

This will create a non-inventory item.

Set Up and Track your Inventory

Setting up and tracking your inventory is easy in QuickBooks. It has all the options that are necessary to set up and manage your inventory. You can track what you have in hand, receive notifications when things are running out, and check the records of what you purchase and sell. Here is a small tutorial of how to set up your inventory and get it running. These steps are easy to understand and follow.

Step 1: Turn on Inventory Tracking

If you have not turned on inventory tracking yet, you need to do so as soon as possible. These settings need to be turned on if you want to add things to your inventory. To start inventory tracking:

1. Go to the Settings option.

2. Click on Company Settings.

3. Click on Sales.

4. Click the Products and services section.

5. Click Edit.

6. Click on the Checkbox near Show Product/Service option.

7. Click on the Checkbox near the Track Quantity option.

8. Click on the Checkbox near Track inventory quantity on hand.

9. Click on Save.

10. Select Done.

Step 2: Add your Inventory Products

Once you have set up your inventory tracking, it is now time to add items to your inventory. It should be noted that all the things that you buy, or sell are not a part of your inventory. You also need to set up the following things in QuickBooks to make your inventory perfect:

Non-Inventory Items

As said above, these are the items that you buy and sell but do not have a stock of. These items generally involve custom order items. This listing also involves installation programs such as nuts, bolts, etc.

Services

In this section, you are supposed to add all the services that you provide to your customers. These include gardening, painting, landscaping, etc.

Bundles

In this section, you should create bundles of services or products that are sold together. For instance, gift baskets that include chocolates, flowers, and wine, etc. By adding these products as bundles, you can save a lot of time, as you won't have to add them individually in your invoice or receipt later.

Step 3: Keep Track of What Sells

Once you have successfully added and set up your inventory products, you need to track them according to their sales. There are two options available for tracking your sales, they are:

1. Create an invoice if you are going to receive the payment later.

2. Create a sales receipt if you receive the payment immediately.

QuickBooks can then reduce what's on hand as compared to the amount present on either the sales receipt or the invoice.

Check what's on hand and what's on order as you work.

Checking what is present in your store and what is still in the form of an invoice, receipt, or sales receipt is simple. Just move your mouse pointer over the quantity that you entered for a product. This will allow you to see more information regarding the product.

You can also set low stock alerts. QuickBooks will sell you a reminder to remind you that things are running low.

Step 4: Restock your Inventory

QuickBooks can automatically tell you whenever it is time to restock. It is possible to order inventory from the program itself. It will keep track of whatever is running low. Similarly, it will also keep track of things that you have ordered and received from the supplier. Once you receive the items, the quantity on hand will increase on its own as well.

Step 5: Use Reports to Check the Status of your Inventory

It is recommended to check the reports to check who the best-sellers are. You can also check the reports to learn about the price of the products, what products you currently have on hand, etc.

Negative Inventory

Negative inventory is a serious problem that can lead to grave errors later. In this section, let us have a look at what this problem is and how to solve it.

Negative Inventory Overview

Negative inventory is usually caused when you enter sales transactions before the corresponding purchase transactions have been entered. In simple words, it means that when you sell inventory items that are currently out of stock.

How to View Negative Inventory

There are different ways to check negative inventory. It generally appears on your Balance Sheet. It also appears on the following report:

IVD or Inventory Valuation Detail Report

The Inventory Valuation Detail Report or the IVD is the only report that can be used to understand the seriousness of your negative inventory. If you have negative inventory, it will show as negative numbers in the QOH or Quantity on Hand column.

To check whether you have a negative inventory problem or not:

1. Click on the Reports menu.

2. Click on Inventory.

3. Click on Inventory Valuation.

Negative Item Listing report

You can use the Negative Item Listing report function if you are using QuickBooks Enterprise 15.0 and later version. In this report, you view the current negative quantities, but this report will not display the past negative quantities.

To check whether you have a negative inventory problem or not:

1. Click on the Reports menu.

2. Click on Inventory.

3. Click on Negative Item Listing.

If you have the QuickBooks Enterprise 2014 version (or earlier) or the QuickBooks Premier version, you can check your negative inventory using Inventory Centre.

To check whether you have a negative inventory problem or not:

1. Click on the Suppliers menu.

2. Click on Inventory Activities.

3. Click on Inventory Center.

4. On the upper left corner of the Inventory Center window, change the filter form Active Inventory to Assembly, to QOH <=Zero.

How to Fix Negative Inventory Problem

In the last section, we saw what negative inventory problem is and how it arises. In this section, let us have a look at some of the methods that can be used to solve this problem.

Reminders

Before trying any of the below-mentioned methods to solve your inventory problem, it is necessary to follow these reminders. By keeping these things in mind, you will be able to avoid loss of data and, in general, frustration. These are simple tips that can be done without any efforts.

Back up your QuickBooks File. Do not overwrite any past backups. Keep all the backups safe and secure so that if you mess up, you can start with a backup once again.

Talk to your accounting professional to check whether the changes that you made are legitimate or not. Some people think that they can solve the negative inventory problem by adjusting the QOH or Quantity on Hand value from negative to positive. But this is false. You also need to change the negative QOH and take precautions to disallow it from happening again.

If you believe that the negative inventory problem is too serious and that it will take a lot of time and effort to repair it, then it is recommended to begin a new data file instead.

Let us now have a look at the variety of solutions that can help you solve the problem of negative inventory.

Your First Transaction for an Item in the Sale

Your inventory reports will turn out to be incorrect if you do no establish an average cost. To rectify this mistake, you need to assure that the earliest dated transaction of a product is a credit card charge, a check, a bill, or Adjust Qty/Value on Hand:

1. Click on the QuickBooks Reports menu.

2. Click on Inventory.

3. Click on the Inventory Valuation summary.

4. Use the QuickZoom function to focus on the item that is displaying wrong values. This can be done by double-clicking the name of the item.

5. A new window called the Inventory Valuation Detail Report will open.

6. QuickZoom on the first Bill.

7. In the new window, change the invoice date.

8. Click Save and close the bill.

9. Repeat these steps until you run out of items.

You sold inventory items without keeping records of the purchases.

Sometimes you may enter bills in the accounts but forget to add the inventory items. If this is the case, then just edit the Bills. To do so, you open the Expense Tab and change the entries. Do remember that changing these may change your inventory expenses as well. This is why it is recommended to consult your accounting professional before beginning this process.

You input purchases and/or adjustments before inputting sales.

If it is possible, change the transaction dates. The dates of the bills should be dated before the invoices.

To do so:

1. Click on the Menu bar and select Reports.

2. Select Inventory.

3. Select the Inventory Valuation Detail.

4. Click on the Dates drop-down menu.

5. Select All.

6. Check out the items to find the items that show the negative amount in the OHC or On Hand Column.

7. Change the dates of invoices.

8. Repeat until no negative entry is left.

How to prevent negative inventory

Preventing negative inventory problems is easy. Just remember not to sell inventory items until you buy them and enter them into QuickBooks.

1. Set up inventory items with an opening balance

2. Create a new inventory item.

3. Add all the necessary information.

4. At the end of the page, add QOH.

5. Also, add the Value. The program will calculate the average cost.

6. If you do not have any units on hand, it is recommended to input purchase before you input a sale.

Use Sales Orders to enter sales for which you do have inventory

To do so, you can either input the customer order as a Sales Order or as an Invoice. If you enter it as an Invoice, just mark the Invoice as Pending. You can do so from the Mark Invoice option from the Edit menu.

1. Buy the inventory items and then input the purchase in your data file.

2. Convert the Sale Order to Invoice.

3. If you used the Pending Invoice method, then mark the Invoice as final. This can be done from the Edit menu as well.

Use Pending Invoices to enter sales for which you do have inventory.

To do this:

1. Input the customer order as an Invoice.

2. Select the Edit option from the menu bar.

3. Click on Mark Invoice as Pending.

4. Buy the items and then enter them as Purchase in your file.

5. Select the Edit option from the menu bar again.

6. Click on Mark Invoice as Final.

7. Adjust the Invoice dates according to your requirement.

CHAPTER SIX

FINANCIAL STATEMENTS

Balance Sheet

A balance sheet is a document that represents the financial status or position of your enterprise at a specific point. The sheet is divided into two sections where one side shows the details of your assets, and the second side shows the equity and liabilities. The two sides should always be equal and balanced, which is why the statement is known as the balance sheet. It is easy to generate balance sheets using QuickBooks.

Let us now have a look at the various types of balance sheets.

Types of Balance Sheets

There are five types of balance sheets that can be created in QuickBooks. Let us have a look at all of them one by one.

Standard

This is a basic balance sheet. In this balance sheet, you can check out your equity, liabilities, and assets for a specific time or date.

Detail

This is the second type of balance sheet that can be generated using QuickBooks. This similar to the Standard balance sheet, but this is more detailed than the previous one. Along with the standard data, it also displays the beginning as well as ending balances of the month. It also displays the transactions that happened during the time.

Summary

This is a short report of all kinds of accounts where you can see the ending balances. It does not show the individual accounts. For instance, a general summary report will show the receivable balance of all the accounts as a total lump sum instead of showing it separately for each individual account.

Previous Year Comparison

This kind of balance sheet is useful to compare the data of the current date and the previous year's date. It can be used to trace the progress or the loss of the firm.

Class

This is another kind of balance sheet that can be created using QuickBooks. In this, the data is displayed in the form of class. This is a method employed by QuickBooks to classify your data. For instance, 'expense class' includes transportation, lodging, and food charges. For an artist, it can also include painting supplies, digital devices, assistant, postage, marketing, etc. It is necessary to assign classes to all kinds of incomes as well as expense transactions else this kind of balance sheet cannot be generated.

Generating a Balance Sheet

Generating a Balance sheet in QuickBooks is simple. To create a balance sheet:

1. Open QuickBooks.

2. Click on the File menu.

3. Click on Reports.

4. Select the Company and Financial menu.

5. Select the type of balance sheet according to your needs and requirements.

Tip

The first displayed balance sheet on the screen is always on the current date. If you want to view the balance sheet of any other date, it is necessary to enter the date in the date field. Click Refresh, and the program will generate a new balance sheet.

Income Statement

An income statement is another form of the statement that is necessary for any business. It is an important financial document. In this statement, a detailed analysis of all your business activities is mentioned. These details can be used to study and determine whether your business is making a profit or is suffering a loss.

It is essential to have this information ready all the time. It can help you to make a choice related to investing as well as spending. By studying the cash flow statement, along with the income statement and the balance statement, you can understand the total financial health of any company.

Many people who have just begun their business do not understand that there exist two kinds of income statements – the single-step version and the multi-step version. In this section, let us have a look at the difference between these two and when to use them. Understanding the difference between these two statements is important, as it will help you avoid an unnecessary hassle in the future. It can also save you a lot of time if you know what to do and how to do it.

What is an Income Statement?

In simple terms, the income statement can be defined as a detailed summary of the income of your enterprise and the expenses spent by the company over a period of time. Business owners generally analyze income statements on the basis of months, quarters, or years.

The period of income statements depends on your needs and requirements. Many people tend to use documents to track their income. For such people, it is recommended to use either monthly statements or quarterly statements. If you are planning to apply for a loan, then you need an annual income statement. QuickBooks can help you produce an income statement according to your needs instantly.

Income Statement Formats

When you generate income statements for your business, you can either use a single-step multi-step statement. These two might appear to be similar, but they are varied. Let us have a look at them one by one.

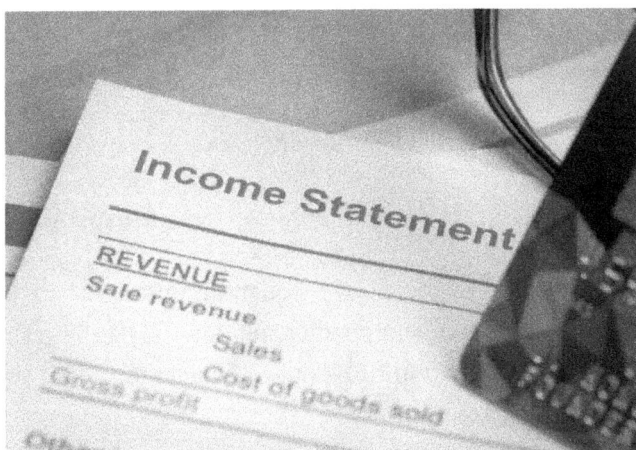

Single-Step Income Statement

Single-step income statements are easy, quick, and effortless as compared to multi-step statements. These statements can be made by deducting the total expenses from the total revenue. The result produced is net income. As it is clear that these reports only have two sections. In one part of the statement, you will find the operating as well as non-operating revenue. In the second section, you will find all the expenses, including the non-operating as well as operating expenses.

Business owners who deal with services generally use a single-step income statement because they do not have any distinct difference between the operating and non-operating contracts. Single-step income statements are easy and convenient, as they are quick and easy to make and compile.

The formula to calculate the single-step income is:

Net income or loss = total revenue - whole expenses

If the result of the above equation turns out to be positive, then you have made a net income. If the result of the above equation turns out to be negative, then you have made a net loss.

Multi-Step Income Statement

Another option to generate income statements is the multi-step income statement. This is quite similar to the single-step income statement, but it is more complex. In this form of the statement, a simple but detailed breakdown of the expenses and revenue is given in two categories. These categories are non-operating and operating.

Another aspect that makes the multi-step income statement different than the single-step income statement is that it also has a third expense category. This category is the 'Cost of Goods Sold.' This category is used to analyze and break down costs.

Operating expenses are directly related to the main activity of any business. These expenses generally include administrative expenses. Non-operating expenses are not directly related to the company and administrative expenses. These are generally related to tax expenses and interest expenses.

The people who generally produce or sell products prefer multi-step income statements. This is because, in such cases, it is crucial to keep the operating and non-operating transactions separate. The multi-step statements are generally used by retailers and manufacturers.

The formula for a multi-step income statement is:

Net income or loss = (total operating revenue + total non-operating revenue) – (total operating expenses + total non-operating expenses + cost of goods sold)

The cost of goods includes all the expenses that are necessary to produce an item. For instance, this may include the machinery, the raw materials, the manufacturing costs, etc. These costs are directly related to the production of your product. All other expenses that are related to the business but are not directly related to the production fall under the operating expenses. Administrative expenses such as wages of your employees are the required amount to run the day-to-day business smoothly.

Revenue and Expenses

An income statement is divided into two distinct categories; these are expenses and revenue. It is important to understand what these categories entail.

Revenue

Revenue is the total income that the company generates. This total income includes:

1. Operating Revenue received from the sale of services as well as goods.

2. The non-operating revenue that is gained in the form of interests acquired on loans. It also includes rent.

3. Revenue generated on sale of long-term assets such as machinery, building, vehicle, etc.

4. Other gains, including successful lawsuits.

5. The gains that are represented on income statements are different than the gross proceeds of any sale. The gains that are displayed on the income statement are the amount by which the proceeds go beyond the asset value in the company catalogs.

If you are accustomed to the accrual accounting method and use it frequently, then you generally report your revenue on the income statement whenever you deal with goods or services. In such cases, the revenue does not depend on whether the payment has been received or not. For instance, if you perform a service, you need to consider the revenue for the income statement when you finish the work, even if you have not been paid yet. The type of payment that you will receive will be presented on the balance sheet. In such sheets, it is possible to include categories such as 'Accounts Receivable' etc., for the amount that your company owes on the balance sheet, but not on the income sheet.

It does not matter if you are paid on the spot or receive the payment sometime later in the future; the results will be the same when you calculate the revenue for the income statement. The revenues can be calculated right after the sale.

This method is useless if you decide to use the cash method of accounting, though. In the cash method of accounting, the revenue is automatically recorded when you receive the cash. For example, if you finish doing a service and give the employee the invoice after 30 days, you will able to record the revenue after a month of finishing the service.

Expenses

It is necessary to include and report all the costs that are required while producing as well as selling an item. It is also recommended to differentiate the expenses into different categories to check how you are spending the money. Some common kinds of expenses include:

1. Operating Expenses: The cost if you have overhead or payroll. Utilities, rent, insurance, publicity, communication, marketing, etc.

2. Non-Operating Expenses: This section includes all the non-core costs, such as interest expenses, an interest that is payable for debt, including loans, bonds, lines of credits, etc.

3. Costs of Goods Sold: The expenses that are directly related to the manufacturing of products. These include inventory costs, purchase of raw material, etc.

4. Losses: Losses are reported on income statements. These include losses that are incurred on lawsuit damages and the sale of assets.

Expenses also change according to the accounting method that you use. For instance, if you use the accrual method, your expenses will be reported as soon as you purchase goods or services on credit or when you receive a bill that is unfinished. In the cash method, the expense will only be recognized when you pay the bill or the invoice for the task.

Maximizing the Multi-Step Income Statement

In the last section, we saw a detailed analysis of how multi-step income statements work. In this section, let us have a look at how multi-step income statements can help you. Multi-step income statements are quite complicated as compared to the single-step statements, but they also provide you with a lot of details and data that normally cannot be accessed in the single-step income statements.

Gross Profit

One of the best things about multi-step income statements is that you can calculate the gross margin or gross profit. Calculating the gross margin is easy. Here is the formula to calculate gross profit:

Gross profit = net sales – cost of goods sold

Here is the formula to calculate the net sales:

Net sales = total sales – sales discounts – sales returns and allowances

Gross profit gives you an idea of how much money you are making after the costs of producing and selling a product are subtracted. It is an important symbol of financial stability. It is important to know how to calculate gross profit as it can help you to decide your pricing strategy. You can also use the gross profit to calculate your gross profit margin ratio. The formula to calculate the gross profit margin ratio is as follows:

Gross profit margin ratio = gross profit ÷ net sales

Gross profit margins are varied, and they change from industry to industry. It is recommended to match or exceed the gross profit margins of your enterprise. If these margins are low, it is recommended to either increase the selling price of your goods, or decrease the production costs.

Operating Income

A multi-step income statement can help you to calculate the operating income as well. The formula to calculate the operating income is as follows:

A multi-step income statement also allows you to calculate your operating income. The formula for operating income is:

Operating income = gross profit − total operating expenses

Here the gross profit allows you to understand how much money you are making from a particular service or good. The operating income allows you to understand how much profit you will gain after deducting all the business functions. For example, you notice a high-profit margin after selling a product. But after subtracting and calculating the operating income, you will see that you are not earning any profit, rather you are breaking even. This shows that your operating expenses are too much, and you need to find a method to cut these back. Operating income often includes the 'Earnings before Interest and Taxes.'

Net Income

Net income is important because it allows you to understand how much you have earned after calculating and incorporating all the expenses. In simple words, operating income decides the 'Earnings before Interest and Taxes' while the net income determines the 'Earnings after Interests and Taxes.' Here is the formula to calculate net income:

Net income = operating income + non-operating revenue – non-operating expenses – income tax expense

Once you have calculated the net income, you can use it to calculate comprehensive income as well. Comprehensive income is great as it can help you incorporate all the income that is related to business. These include the income that is generally not a part of the net income.

Business owners and firm managers can use the comprehensive income to incorporate the unrealized gains and losses. For example, the owner can incorporate the gains and losses from the firm's investments made in mutual funds or stocks. The market value of the stock needs to be higher than the amount that the owner bought it for if he or she wants to see a high comprehensive income. If the market value is lower than the purchase price, the owner will experience loss. Here is the formula to calculate comprehensive income:

Comprehensive income = net income + other comprehensive income – other comprehensive expenses

Formatting your Income Statement

Whether it is necessary to format your income statements or not solely depends on how and why you use them. For instance, if you plan to use the income statements only for internal use, then it does not matter whether you format them or not. You just need to keep the elements mentioned above accurate and correct. You can use any simple template available online to create your income statement.

In many cases, specific kinds of income statements are required. For instance, when you want to apply for a loan, banks generally ask for income statements that have been formatted in a particular and specific way. It is thus recommended to check the requirements before submitting an income statement.

This is another reason why the multi-step income statement is better than a single-step income statement. It does not matter if your expenses and revenues are straightforward; the multi-step income statement will still help you.

If you are used to a single-step income statement, you may find it difficult to use the multi-step income statement format. But, if your bank asks for it, then you will have to produce it anyhow. It is difficult to go from a single-step income statement format to a multi-step income statement format, but vice versa is simple. So it is recommended to use a multi-step income statement format whenever possible.

Compiling Income statement

As said above, income statements are absolutely critical documents for your company. It is necessary to generate at least one accurate income statement per quarter. This will help you understand the financial condition, the loss, the growth, and the value of your company. When an accurate and timely income statement is used along with a cash flow statement and a balance sheet, it can help you understand and manage the growth of your organization.

Cash Flow Statements

Cash flow can be compared to the fuel compartment of your vehicle. If you fill the compartment with fuel, it will run out slowly whenever you drive your vehicle. But if you drive too much or too quickly, you will run out of fuel. Your mission should be keeping your fuel tank full all the time. It should have at least some fuel in it all the time. Similarly, cash flow is the movement of cash in and out of your expenses. Positive cash flow is good for the company, while negative cash flow is bad for the company. It is necessary to maintain positive cash flow as much as possible.

Why is Cash Flow Important to Your Business?

For small (and many times large) business owners, positive cash flow is the ultimate goal. The owner should be able to make more money than he or she spends. While this equation sounds simple, many profitable businesses often run into cash flow issues. It is often difficult to balance the business expenses such as rent, wages, machinery, revenue, etc. with seasonal negative cash flow.

It is necessary for a small business not only to achieve a positive cash flow but to maintain it as well. In simple terms, it is necessary to check where your cash goes every month. Similarly, it is also necessary to understand how much cash you require to run the basic functions of your company.

To understand what cash flow is, it is first necessary to have a look at the cash flow statement. It is also important to learn how to read cash flow statements. This can help you to know what problems generally arise in similar businesses and how to avoid them.

What is a Cash Flow Statement?

A statement of cash flow or a cash flow statement is a statement that tracks the 'money coming in' and the 'money going out' of your enterprise. This statement records how much money your enterprise has on hand and what the liquidity of the enterprise is. It is necessary for public companies to release their cash flow statements at least every quarter.

What does a Cash Flow Statement consist Of?

Cash flow statements, income statements, and balance sheets are necessary as they help you to understand the financial condition of your company. But not many business owners know or understand how these three are connected.

The balance sheet is a record of all your finances. It is generally divided into three sections, which are liabilities, assets, and equity. The cash balance calculated using this statement is present on the balance sheet under the asset section.

The income statement is a record of the revenue, profit, loss, and expenses of an enterprise. It is good to gain insight into the financial condition of the company and whether it is gaining profit or not. The income statement is used to calculate the net income while the net income is used to calculate the cash flow. Any income that is not in the form of cash, including depreciation, affects the net income as well. These incomes go into the cash-flow statement as well.

It is thus clear that you need to have a comprehensive knowledge of all three statements if you want to understand the financial condition of your company from all angles. The cash flow statement and the balance sheet are focused on the management of the finances of your company in terms of assets and structure. The income statement is related to the central operations, which are responsible for the generation of income for your company.

Cash flow and profits are both important for your business. If you want your business to be successful and profitable in the long term, you need to have positive cash flow along with a good percentage of profit. But remember, profit does not equal cash flow as they are two distinct terms.

Cash Inflow and Outflow on your Cash Flow Statement

Businesses fail due to a variety of reasons, but one of the main reasons why they fail is because people do not understand cash flow, or they do not understand how to manage the cash flow. This is why it is necessary to understand cash inflows and outflows that are present in the cash flow statement. If you understand them and manage them properly, you will be able to keep your business running successfully.

Cash inflow is the money that goes into your company. This money comes in from a variety of sources; for instance, it can come from sales, from investments, or from financing as well. Cash outflow is the opposite of cash inflow. Cash outflow means when money goes out of your company for a variety of reasons, including disbursements, and payments to sellers, vendors, etc. If you want your company to be healthy and financially stable, your cash outflow should always be lower than the cash inflow.

You can find a variety of options on your cash flow statements. These include investing activity, operating activity, and financing activity. When the total cash gained from all these three activities is added together, you can count the overall change in cash for a particular point in time. If this amount is added to the opening cash balance, you will be able to calculate the closing cash balance.

The Difference between Cash Flow and Profit

As said above, cash flow and profit may appear to be the same thing, but they are two distinct entities in the world of accounting. To see the difference between profits and cash flow, you should compare a cash flow statement with an income statement.

The biggest difference between cash flow statements and income statements is that income statement is generally based on accrual accounting, while the cash flow statement is generally based on cash basis accounting.

Even if you do not manage your financial reporting on your own, it is still necessary to understand the basics of cash-based accounting and accrual accounting and the difference between them. This way, you can decide which form of accounting is the best for you. It is also necessary to understand that if your sales are lower than $25 million per year, you can use any of the above-mentioned methods.

Cash-Based Accounting

In the case of cash-based, revenue is mentioned when it is received, while expenses are mentioned when they are paid. This type of accounting will not recognize accounts payable and accounts receivable. Many small businesses use this method of accounting because it is quick and can be maintained with ease. It is simple to check when a transaction has been done and how much cash your business has on hand by simply checking out your bank balance quickly.

Accrual Accounting

Accrual accounting is far more complex than cash-based accounting. In this type of account, the revenues and expenses both are recorded when they are earned and not when they are paid. This means that the payment may happen immediately or after months, but the expenses and revenues will be recorded immediately.

For instance, if you pay $300 for a magazine subscription, there will be a $300 outflow from your cash flow statement. But, on the other hand, your income statement will divide the $300 into different accounting periods. These will usually be quarterly or monthly.

Imagine that you have just started a new company. After a year, you start having some cash flow issues despite your business being profitable. If you are a small business owner, you probably have invoices to collect credits and the remaining amounts from your customers. It is a well-known fact that customers rarely pay on time. Thus, even though the income statement recorded a profit for your company, you were still short on cash all the time. As you did not have cash, you could not pay your vendors on time. This is because you were not able to manage cash inflow and outflow properly — the relationship between cash flow and profit change according to the nature of your business. Sometimes you can see a lot of profit even when the cash flow is slow or inconsistent.

This means that cash flow is the money that constantly moves in or out of your business at any time. Compared to this, profit is the amount that remains after all the expenses have been deducted.

How to Read a Cash Flow Statement

Reading a cash flow statement is not a difficult job. To read it efficiently, you should break it down into the following equation:

Operating activities + financing activities+ investing activities = cash on hand

Let us now have a look at the various terms present in the above equation one by one.

Operating Activities

These activities are also known as operating cash flow. These record two things - the money you spend on a daily basis or the money you made on a daily basis. It is the money that your enterprise gains from any constant regular business activities. These activities include manufacturing, selling products, providing services, etc. This is considered to be a highly accurate assessment of how much money you gained from core business activities.

Investment Activities

These are also known as cash flow from investing activities. These assets generally include machinery, equipment, vehicles, property, investment securities, and furnishings. With time, your business becomes capable enough to pay for these investments with the help of the income created through their daily operations.

Financing Activities

Financing is the amount of cash that is either received or paid to lenders, investors, and creditors. In publicly traded companies, this section is also related to cash flow from the sale of stocks and bonds, repayment of the debt, and payment of dividends.

The cash flow equation is essential to understand the cash flow of your company.

What Causes Cash Flow Problems?

A lot of businesses have failed because the owners could not understand the difference between managing cash flow and making money. Many times, cash flow becomes a challenge because income is rarely constant, and expenses rarely sporadic. Both these affect your cash flow, but sales are never a problem related to cash flow. Sales problems are generally associated with products or sales.

There is a problem in the cash flow when the sales happen, but cash gets stuck in either account receivable or inventory. So while the sales are good, you do not have cash in hand to pay for other commodities and vendors. In simple terms, the cash is flowing in, but it is not flowing into the bank.

It is recommended to control your accounts receivable carefully as it will help you increase cash flow. There are a variety of ways through which you can get paid quickly, but many times even these methods may not work. Tracking late payments is a time-consuming task that often requires a lot of effort and money.

The best way to avoid past due receivable from growing is not to let them pile up ever. But this is not possible all the time. Some companies thus try to find some business financing options that allow them to get out of the crunch for a while. But even this can backfire sometimes.

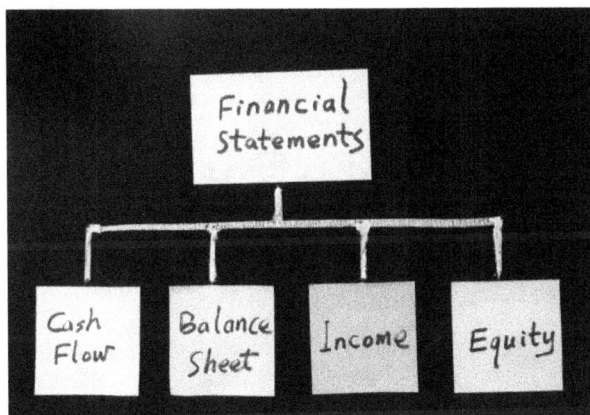

CHAPTER SEVEN

BOOKKEEPING WITH QUICKBOOKS

QuickBooks ProAdvisor

The departments of finance and accounting are always the central unit of any business. If your current properties, liabilities, and assets are confusing and are frankly a mess, and you do not know what your current financial status is, then it can lead to drastic results. It can even ruin your business forever.

A good accountant or team of accountants can make or break a business. To keep everything simple and free of chaos, it is recommended to hire a good accountant to manage your finances. The accounts are responsible for managing the financial aspects of any business. They maintain the general ledger and financial statements as well. They study the cost of operation, budgeting, and income tax returns as well.

If you are currently looking to update your business and make everything automatic and let everyone have access to the information related to business remotely, then instead of hiring a regular accountant, it is recommended to use QuickBooks ProAdvisor version. This program will help you to get a clear view of your current financial status and will also help you to understand the position in the market.

QuickBooks ProAdvisor can help you in a lot of ways. Successful businesses are rarely stagnant. They need to grow to become successful. It is necessary to hire people who can understand your business, the goals of your business, and what you are trying to achieve. Such people can then offer you proper financial advice that can help your business to grow exponentially.

Regular accountants do not have in-depth knowledge regarding QuickBooks products. This is why hiring a QuickBooks ProAdvisor is a far better option than hiring a regular accountant. A QuickBooks ProAdvisor is an experienced, well-trained, and certified professionals who can not only set up your accounts and the program but can also manage both of these things efficiently. QuickBooks ProAdvisors are experts in handling the desktop versions, as well as the online version of QuickBooks.

Every QuickBooks ProAdvisor needs to undergo strict training. They need to pass a series of tests that come after intensive training offered by Intuit. Once they pass these tests, they are certified by Intuit. The ProAdvisors need to re-take certain tests annually to update their knowledge. This keeps them up-to-date and the most trustworthy experts regarding QuickBooks.

A QuickBooks ProAdvisor can help you in a variety of ways. He or she is an expert in a lot of accounting operations, including bookkeeping. They can help you with the most complex tasks and will also help you solve the simplest of problems as well.

Here is a list of reasons that prove why it is recommended to get a QuickBooks ProAdvisor for your business if you want to achieve great success.

An Expert in QuickBooks Setup

As said above, a QuickBooks ProAdvisor is expert in everything related to QuickBooks. It is one of the most common and frequently used accounting software used by a variety of businesses all over the world. It is used to manage bills, expenses, incomes, sales, and can also study the profit levels by analyzing the complete payrolls and costs.

While using QuickBooks is quite easy, some people may find it difficult, especially in the beginning. If you do not want to be bogged down by accounting terms, it is recommended to use the proAdvisor version of QuickBooks. The ProAdvisor will do all the technical work related to QuickBooks. They can solve the problems related to accounts and can also help you understand and track cash flow and revenue as well. They can also help you if you ever run into any problem while dealing with QuickBooks.

Stay Up- To- Date on Tax Laws

QuickBooks ProAdvisors are supposed to stay updated all the time. They also tend to work hard to keep themselves updated about tax and federal changes as well as future regulations. He or she constantly study the accounting rules and regulations that are essential to keep accounting operations correct and error-free. The ProAdvisor can help you to understand the laws and can help you to tailor the objectives of your business accordingly.

ProAdvisors also try to find changes that can help you to lower inventory costs and increase revenue as well. This is essential for the growth of your business.

Provide Financial Advice and Insights

QuickBooks ProAdvisors are supposed to keep themselves updated about business development data and strategic planning options as well. They can provide you with trustworthy and essential advice that can be used to decide the best cash flow pattern, the best accounting structure, and the best financial plan that can help you to keep your business at the forefront.

They can also guess the accounting trends and other similar indicators that can help your accounting system. These are essential as they can improve the financial stability of your enterprise.

They determine accounting trends and other indicators to improve the accounting system and the company's financial position.

Businesses generally tend to grow a lot when the owners use the advice and insights provided by QuickBooks ProAdvisors. They are trained to prepare proper financial plans and can also forecast the expenses that you may have to face in the future. These things can help you to make good decisions in the future.

Training for Accounting Staff

QuickBooks ProAdvisors are experts in their field because they undergo extensive training related to

QuickBooks. This makes them great coaches for other accountants as well. They can help the accounting team of any enterprise to learn the intricacies of the program. This way, the accounting team and the ProAdvisor can work efficiently together. The collaboration of the team can help you make better decisions. A well-trained team can also help you avoid mistakes and errors that can ruin a company.

The accounting team of a firm is generally led by the QuickBooks ProAdvisor. He or she coaches them and teaches them how to correct deductions, tax mistakes, and credits as well. With the help of the professional support provided by the QuickBooks ProAdvisors, the accountants can work on profits and losses, payments process, and various other accounting-related functions in an effortless, timesaving, and hassle-free manner.

Focus on Growth

One of the best things about QuickBooks ProAdvisor is that he or she can understand and explain the total costs, expenses, accounts receivables, and payables as well. They can accurately guess the taxes and can help you fill the monthly payroll tax to prevent penalties.

QuickBooks ProAdvisors can assess and identify the sections that need adjustments so that the profiles can be boosted. They work as per the accounting procedures and benchmarks. They do this to keep the fiscal health of your business intact.

QuickBooks ProAdvisors can help business owners in a variety of ways. Their help is not only restricted to planning and preparing tax. The ProAdvisors can also help the owners to expand the company, to instill good money management practices, and maintain good cash flow and tax efficiency as well. He or she does this almost without any effort.

The evaluations done by QuickBooks ProAdvisors are based on specific parameters. They can help you save time as well as money. QuickBooks ProAdvisors generate reports right out of the accounting program. They can make plans for required KPIs. They can help you keep your accounts smooth and effortless.

Along with this, the QuickBooks ProAdvisors can also guess the risks in need of mitigation. This way, the business leaders do not need to care about mitigation and can instead concentrate on their work and other aspects of the company as well.

Summary

It is necessary for every business to have a QuickBooks ProAdvisor in their team. He or she can make the complex accounting process easy, which will ensure steady growth. He or she can help you understand and interpret the financial aspects and status of your company in a better way. This will help you to understand your tax revenue, and manage your cash flow efficiently.

It is thus a great decision to seek the services of a QuickBooks ProAdvisor. This can help you to form a good business plan that can make your company a huge success.

Choosing the Right Plan

If you are a new business owner, or if you a seasoned entrepreneur, it is necessary for you to have an accounting system that will help you take your business to the next level. It is crucial that your bookkeeping software should be user-friendly. It should be able to handle all your transactions and deals. It should be up-to-date and should have all the features that are necessary in the modern world in an affordable range.

While a multitude of programs is available that can be used for accounting and bookkeeping, only a few of them can boast of possessing all the qualities mentioned above. One such brilliant accounting solution is QuickBooks. This program is great for a variety of businesses. It can help you track your inventory, can help you create reports, and can help you understand your taxes if you are self-employed, etc. Thus, QuickBooks is highly recommended for everyone who owns a business.

While QuickBooks is a versatile software, there are multiple iterations available in the QuickBooks family. It is thus quite difficult to choose the correct version that will match your needs perfectly.

QuickBooks Desktop

QuickBooks desktop has been on the market since the 1990s. It is one of the eldest and trustworthy brands in the world of accounting. A new version of QuickBooks has become highly popular in recent times. This version is called the QuickBooks Online version. It is, in a way, a stripped-down version of the desktop version. While it is true that it does not have a lot of bells and whistles like the desktop version, but it still has all the functions that are necessary for accounting and bookkeeping purposes.

In this chapter, let us have a look at different versions of QuickBooks one by one. In this particular section, we will look at QuickBooks Desktop and QuickBooks Online specifically.

QuickBooks Online

QuickBooks Online, or QBO, as it is popularly known, is a cloud-based system that has become highly popular in recent times. One of the best things about this version is that it is extremely flexible, which allows users to access the files of their company from anywhere. If your device has Internet capabilities, you will be able to access

QuickBooks Online easily. You do not need to wait for your accountants or bookkeepers to send you your files as you can download them or view them from anywhere if you have a device that is capable of connecting to the Internet.

Another factor that makes QBO or QuickBooks Online really great is that it does not require any kind of installation. This means you do not need to download anything to use it. It is totally web-hosted. You just need a device connected to the Internet. All your data is collected and stored on a totally secure cloud service. Similarly, if you ever want to update your data, you can do it with ease using your web browser. This makes QuickBooks Online a safe, timesaving, effortless, and flexible option for all users.

One more feature that makes QuickBooks Online really flexible is that it allows multiple users to use the program while accessing it from multiple devices simultaneously. You do not need to pay extra for these users. There exists a user limit, though.

Within the platform, it is possible for the users to access the files of the company together. But it is recommended to avoid changing the files simultaneously as it may lead to confusion and errors. This option should be used only to view files and data.

User Limits

As said above, multiple users can use the QuickBooks Online edition simultaneously, but it has its limitations as well. All the versions of QuickBooks have different user limits. The most cost-effective version of QuickBooks Online is called Simple Start. It has all the basic features. The next subscription plan is QuickBooks Online Essential, and the most advanced and expensive subscription plan for QuickBooks Online is QuickBooks Online Plus. Each level of subscription offers different features and different user limits as well. This is why it is recommended to have a look at the features, functions, and limitations of all the editions before subscribing to any edition.

But don't worry, if you ever feel that the edition or the plan that you have subscribed is not suitable for your needs, then you can change, i.e., upgrade or downgrade the plans by contacting Intuit immediately.

Intuit decided to start the online version of QuickBooks because it realized that a lot of professionals were demanding such a version. As the world is changing rapidly, people want to stay connected all the time. They want to stay connected with their data, and they believe that they should be able to access it anytime, anywhere. This desire is also closely related to the desire of having a SAAS or software as a service. People who want a

SAAS believe that paying to upgrade software applications on a system does not make any sense. It is thus no wonder that this version has become so popular among customers, users, and professionals all around the world. It has become a boon for small business owners who are generally on the road for a long time. It is true that it is slightly expensive as compared to the purchase of the desktop version, but it is surely worth it. If the features of QuickBooks Online is compared with other QuickBooks products, it is clear that it has all the features and more of QuickBooks Pro 2011. This makes it highly suitable for users who indulge in various vocations and businesses.

One of the best things about using the online version of QuickBooks is that you do not need to worry about your data. Your data is stored online on the cloud, which means that it will stay safe no matter what. It will never crash. It is continuously backed up and can be accessed from anywhere and at any time. You just need a device with an Internet connection to access your data. This flexibility and ease of use have made QuickBooks Online a highly popular program.

Versions

Currently, there are five different versions of QuickBooks Online that are available on the market. Out of these five, we have already seen the first three versions briefly. The following are the five versions of QuickBooks Online:

1. Online Simple Start

2. Online Essentials

3. Online Plus

4. Online Essentials with Payroll

5. Online Plus with Payroll

Let us now have a look at all these versions one by one.

Simple Start

As said above, the Simple Start version is the least expensive version of QuickBooks Online. It is the most basic version of QuickBooks, and it does not have a lot of features. It is generally considered to be of no use for many businesses. You cannot import the QuickBooks Desktop version files into it. Similarly, it does not allow you to make invoices, conduct online banking, does not allow you to make bills, does not allow you to use a purchase order, it has no option to take company snapshots, and it does not allow you to track time either. These options are quite affordable, but as it does not offer a lot of features, many people generally tend to go for upgrades immediately. This is a good starting point to learn the basics, but it is recommended to use a more advanced version.

Online Essentials

This is the 'standard' version of the accounting service. It can be used to run a simple normal business. It is true that you cannot create a bill by the customer, but it is still a highly suitable version. Other features that are not available in this version include multiple location tracking, purchase order, class tracking, inventory tracking, planning, and budgeting. These features are available in the Online Plus version of QuickBooks Online. If you have a product-based service, it is recommended to go for Online Plus instead of using the Essentials. This will help you to keep things simple.

Many accountants and experts agree with the above point. If you have simple accounting needs, then subscribing to QuickBooks Online is the best option for you. If you believe that you require a lot of complex accounting needs, then it is recommended to go for the desktop version of the program instead. The desktop version is well suited to handle the heavy load.

Tip

If you ever decide to cancel your subscription of QuickBooks Online, the software will still keep your data for a month. You can export this data to either a spreadsheet or to the Desktop version of the program. This data cannot be changed or edited on the cloud. If you do not download the data before a year, the data will disappear, and you will not be able to access it afterward.

QuickBooks Desktop vs. QuickBooks Online

The online version of QuickBooks is great for all small-scale businesses. This version is also good for consultants as well as freelancers. These people generally need a service that is simple and flexible. QuickBooks Online provides them these functions.

As mentioned above, many different users can use and access the cloud-based software together in real-time. Another great thing about this version is that the data is backed up and synced automatically to the cloud.

These are some of the features that are available in QuickBooks Online but are not available in QuickBooks Desktop.

- You can upload and backup documents, files, and images from a mobile device or tablet.

- You can send and schedule automatic transactions.

- You can auto register banks.

- You can download the bank transactions automatically at night.

- The option of custom splitting, which is based on percentage or amount.

- You can also assign location rules and classes.

- You can audit logs and review the actions.

- You can track changes as well.

- You can give seven different names to the customer.

- You can delay credits and charges for any non-posting transactions that will be billed later.

- Multi-line journal entries are available for Accounts Receivable and Account Payable.

- Multi-fiscal year budgeting capabilities.

- It can be integrated seamlessly with many different third-party apps such as Bill.com, Tsheets, and Expensify.

- Free 30-day trial period

QuickBooks Desktop

QuickBooks Desktop has a multitude of benefits and solutions that make it one of the best accounting and bookkeeping apps for any business. There are some problems associated with QuickBooks Desktop; for instance, you need to buy a user license for each and every individual user. So, unlike QuickBooks Online, multiple users cannot use it simultaneously unless you are ready to pay this extra amount. Each separate user and each separate computer will have to pay a separate license fee as well. This is why some people do not use QuickBooks Desktop.

There are three different versions of QuickBooks Desktop available on the market; they are called the QuickBooks Pro, QuickBooks Premier, and QuickBooks Enterprise. Some features and tools are available in only Enterprise and Premier versions and are not available in the Pro version. A detailed analysis of these three versions is available in the next section.

QuickBooks Online vs. QuickBooks Desktop

The Desktop version of QuickBooks is extremely robust and full of features. It has a lot of product-based as well as accounting features. This is why companies that are focused on products generally use the Desktop version to manage their accounts. This is especially true in the case of small businesses. This system is great for financial tracking and inventory tracking, as well. These two are important as they allow users to understand the profitability of sales and expenses. They can also help you to forecast things that generally require users to purchase third party applications and add-ons.

Features

Here is a list of major features that are only available in the QuickBooks Desktop version but are not available in QuickBooks Online version.

The following features are available via QuickBooks Desktop but are not supported via QBO.

Reporting Capabilities

1. It offers industry-specific reporting

2. It offers impeccable business planning and forecasting

3. You can create balance sheet by class options as well

4. It offers multiple customization offers for footer and header

Another great feature that the Desktop version offers is Scheduled Reporting. This feature was added to the program in 2017. It enables users to create scheduled reports. This can help the user to create scheduled reports which can be sent using email directly. This is brilliant for the finances of the company. It also helps you to save a lot of time and effort in the long term.

Accounting Benefits

- It can print the Form 1099-MISC

- It can create the Produce Period Copy

- It offers a variety of client data review options and tools

- It offers backup and restores options for accountants

- It can clean files

- It can correct unapplied payments and credits

- It can send you reminders to deposit undeposited funds

- It can fix sales tax errors

Data Entry

- It can generate Invoice Batches

- It can create batch transactions

- It can customize billing rate levels

- The payroll can take in batched timesheets as well

Inventory Features

The Desktop version of QuickBooks has many different inventory features; they include:

- Sales Order Tracking

- Unit of Measurement Inventory

- Valuation Method for Average Cost of Inventory

- Purchase Order Process Receiving Capabilities

- Custom Inventory Reorder Scheduling

A lot of custom features have been added to QuickBooks Desktop that is similar to the features of QuickBooks Online. The main motive behind this is to make the Desktop version as user-friendly as possible. This way, it becomes highly suitable for all users who do not want to handle a difficult to use software but do not want to forgo on the robustness of the program either.

How to Choose?

The choice between QuickBooks Desktop and QuickBooks Online is a difficult one. There are many pros and cons of both the products that should be considered before buying any version. Here is a small list of aspects and areas that you can consider before making a choice for your business. Let us have a look at them one by one:

Customization

QuickBooks Desktop has a lot of customization options. For instance, you can customize expense categories, forms, and can also track employee mileage as well. These customization options are not available in QuickBooks Online.

Cost

QuickBooks Online is great because it has a 30-day trial period, but after 30 days, the user needs to pay a subscription fee, which is usually monthly. Compared to this, you need to pay only a one-time fee to use the desktop version. The cost of the product solely depends on the product that you have selected. It can either be Pro, Premier, or Enterprise.

Automated Functions

QuickBooks Online is a great option for people who only deal with things such as downloading bank transactions, customer billing, and payment processing. Most of these things are generally done manually using QuickBooks Desktop. Nowadays, thanks to the new update, QuickBooks Desktop now offers automatic reporting as well.

Accessibility

QuickBooks Online can be accessed from any device in the world that is connected with the Internet. Compared to this, QuickBooks Desktop can only be accessed using the device on which it has been installed. The device needs to have the license for this access as well. QuickBooks Online is based on the cloud; this means that it can be accessed remotely as well.

QuickBooks Desktop to QuickBooks Online

Intuit is enabling more and more people to use QuickBooks Online. This is because the business keeps on evolving, and a lot of business now happens on the cloud. People who generally use QuickBooks Desktop can shift to QuickBooks Online using the following option:

1.   Open QuickBooks Desktop

2.   Click on Company.

3. Click on Export Company File to QuickBooks Online

4. Click on Help

5. Click on Update QuickBooks

6. Click on All updates from the Update Now Window

7. Click on Get Updates

8. Click on Close

9. Click on File Menu

10. Click Exit.

11. Restart QuickBooks and let the installation process finish. This process usually takes around 15 minutes to finish, but it may take even longer if you haven't updated for a long time.

12. Enter your login details for QuickBooks Online.

13. Click on Agree to Terms of Service.

14. Click Submit.

15. Choose the online company you want to import the data into. You can also generate a new company.

16. Click OK.

17. You will soon receive an email from QuickBooks.

Which Version is best for you?

As it is clear from above that the QuickBooks Desktop version and the QuickBooks Online version are quite different and have their own sets of pros and cons. The decision solely depends on which version to get.

Once again, the QuickBooks Desktop version is designed for people who want to use customized budgeting and reporting options. Similarly, it is also great for users who do not want to pay a monthly subscription charge. The users who prefer desktop versions usually do not care about online access and remote access to the books. They do not care if they cannot access their books all the time.

It should be noted that all the businesses do not need all the functions and features that QuickBooks Desktop has to offer. This is okay. If you do not know which version to choose, it is recommended to try out the 30-Day Trial for QuickBooks Online version. You can also use other applications to fill in the gaps that the QuickBooks Online version has. It should be noted that most of the third-party apps will charge you some money. They generally have an annual or a monthly subscription amount.

QuickBooks Desktop Versions and Others

As said above, there are multiple versions of QuickBooks Desktop. In this section, let us have a look at these versions in detail. Along with these versions, this section will also cover some other versions of QuickBooks.

In the beginning, Intuit, the parent company of QuickBooks, offered only one version of QuickBooks. But with time, the technology has evolved, and now Intuit has created a variety of versions of the program. These various options include QuickBooks Mac, QuickBooks Online, QuickBooks Simple Start, QuickBooks Standard, QuickBooks Pro, QuickBooks Enterprise, and QuickBooks Premier. There are also other varieties, such as industry-specific versions of QuickBooks. These versions are often customized according to the enterprise or industry. If you do not want to use a specific industrial version of QuickBooks, you can also use a regular version of QuickBooks and customize it according to your needs and requirements.

Due to a multitude of options that are available, users may find it quite daunting to select a version of QuickBooks that will fulfill their needs. This section will help you learn how to choose between different versions of QuickBooks.

As said above, choosing between different versions of QuickBooks is difficult. Many people think that the more money you pay, the better suited the program will be. Many times, the most expensive programs have a lot of functions and features. But if you do not need such features, it is recommended to avoid such a version. There are only two things that you need to consider when buying QuickBooks. These two things are your needs and requirements. For instance, if you do a lot of daily transactions and financial deals as well, you will need a good accountant. If such a person decides to use the simplest and least expensive version of QuickBooks, his or her business will suffer a lot. Similarly, a person has just started a business and is looking to expand it by using accounting software and decided to get the most expensive. This person, too, will suffer the fate of a misguided choice. Both these people will not only waste a lot of money and effort, but they will also lose a lot of important time as well. It is thus recommended to make choices correctly.

But then how do you make a choice when there are so many options available on the market? Is it worth paying the extra amount to buy Premier? Is QuickBooks Online sufficient for my business, or should I get something else? These and many other questions are quite popular related to QuickBooks. If you, too, are plagued by the question of choice, this section will help you make the correct decision regarding which version of QuickBooks to buy.

There are many different versions of QuickBooks, and each industry or enterprise needs a different version. But almost all businesses can make do with QuickBooks Pro, as it is a good combination of features, ease of use, and affordable. But it is still recommended to think wisely before choosing this version. QuickBooks is not cheap software, and many versions of the program retail for several hundred dollars. If you buy a QuickBooks version without checking whether it suits your company or not, you will lose a lot of money.

This section will try to cover all the different varieties of QuickBooks in brief. This brief information regarding the QuickBooks versions will help make your choice quickly and effortlessly. It will also provide you multiple options according to your needs or requirements.

QuickBooks Versions

Let us now have a look at the different versions of QuickBooks that are currently available on the market.

QuickBooks for Mac

This has been placed here because this is the easiest decision to make. If your company uses predominantly (or perhaps) only Mac operating system, then you need to use QuickBooks Mac. There are currently no other QuickBooks options available from Intuit that can be used on Macs (except the Online version, which can be used on any device with an Internet connection). QuickBooks Mac is quite different from any other desktop version of QuickBooks because it is, in a way, a software package that contains a multitude of different products that are not available in other Desktop packages offered by QuickBooks. Barring the QuickBooks Online and QuickBooks Mac, all other versions of QuickBooks run on Windows. QuickBooks Mac has been specially devised and created in such a way that it can integrate and work properly with the Mac interface and framework. You can use the different functions, modules, features, and sections of this software without forgoing the Mac features. In the beginning, QuickBooks Mac was complicated and difficult to use. It was not user-friendly at all. But with time, Intuit has developed far better products. Now the Mac version of QuickBooks looks like a proper Mac application and works like one as well. The new editions of QuickBooks Mac can be integrated with various other services, including iCal for calendar-related features and MobileMe for backups and restoration processes.

Another positive factor with QuickBooks is that it is possible to share data from QuickBooks Desktop (Windows) to QuickBooks Mac and vice versa. This is a great option when your accountant uses QuickBooks Mac, and you use QuickBooks Windows.

While Intuit does not have a Premier version for QuickBooks Mac, the regular version will suffice the needs of common users. But if you need extremely advanced capabilities and functionalities, then you need to get a Windows PC and use the Windows version of QuickBooks. If you do not want to get a Windows PC, you can also try a Windows Emulator to use the Windows program.

QuickBooks Pro

QuickBooks Pro is perhaps the most downloaded and highly popular version of QuickBooks. This is because it is affordable, it is cost-effective, and it contains almost all the commonly required functions and tools that are necessary for day-to-day accounting. If you really want to take your business to the next level, then QuickBooks Pro can help you a lot. If you want more capabilities, then it is recommended to go QuickBooks Premier instead.

QuickBooks Pro has a variety of features that are explained below:

- It can help you track your expenses.

- It can help you track your bills.

- It can help you print checks.

- It can help you track sales.

- It can help you create new and track customer accounts.

- It has good payroll management capabilities.

- It can generate invoices and reports.

- It can create estimates.

- Using a service, it can accept credit cards as well.

- You can do batch invoicing using this QuickBooks version.

- Three users can use the program simultaneously.

- You can track expenses as well as time for specific clients with ease.

QuickBooks Premier

QuickBooks Premier is a highly advanced version of QuickBooks. It is more focused on vertical industries and enterprises. Usually, contractors, general business owners, manufacturers, wholesale sellers, people who offer professional services, and people in retail use QuickBooks Premier. This version of QuickBooks is highly customizable, and you can change a lot of details in it. For instance, even the name of the objects changes according to the industry. Thus, Customers become Donors if you use this version for a non-profit organization. This makes QuickBooks Premier a versatile and flexible application.

Along with the features present in QuickBooks Pro, the QuickBooks Premier has some more features. These include:

- It can help you create a business plan

- It can help you forecast expenses and sales

- It can help you track balance sheet by class

- It has an option of industry-specific reporting

QuickBooks Enterprise

QuickBooks Enterprise is Intuit's foray into the large, industrial level business world. The Enterprise version of QuickBooks has the option to have more data sets.

These data sets fall under the range of 14,500 limits to 1,000,000 limits. This is absolutely necessary for large businesses. Generally, large businesses have a large number of accountants as well. This range can help the accountants do their jobs with ease.

The Enterprise version of QuickBooks is great for companies where more users need to use the program. It also offers other functionalities such as more audit trails and good integration capabilities. You can integrate the program with various other business systems.

This version is surely expensive, but if you really have a huge industry, then it is recommended to get this version.

This is the best accounting software for you if you have a large organization. Using other versions of QuickBooks will only waste your time, as they will not be able to handle your operations properly. Thus, instead of wasting time, money, and effort on other accounting software, it is recommended to get QuickBooks Enterprise immediately.

How to Decide Which QuickBooks to Buy

Until now, we have covered the variety of versions of QuickBooks that are available on the market. In the last section, we saw how to choose between QuickBooks Online and QuickBooks Desktop. If you have decided to go with QuickBooks Desktop, this section will help you choose between the three versions of the program. All the different versions of QuickBooks software have their own pros and cons. It is thus your duty to make a list of your requirements and the needs of your firm before making a decision. You should also check out all the features of the programs once again and then finally select a version of QuickBooks that will suit your requirements. Avoid getting something too basic or equally something too advanced. This section will help you narrow down your choices significantly.

If you are a Mac user, then the best option for you is obviously QuickBooks Mac. But it is not your only choice. You can also use QuickBooks Online. If you want to use QuickBooks Premier or QuickBooks Pro on a Mac, it is possible. You just need to install a Windows Emulator on your Mac. But it is recommended to use a dedicated Windows PC instead.

If you need a lot of remote access and want to access your data any time anywhere, then QuickBooks Online is the best option for you. This is a great option for organizations that are quick-paced and contemporary. This version is really popular with people who like to have access to their data all the time.

Nowadays, some other versions of QuickBooks have started offering the anytime, anywhere data option as well. For instance, QuickBooks Pro now offers a service through which you can switch on mobile and remote data access. You just need to pay a small monthly service fee to use this feature. But the overall price to use this feature is high, but if you need anywhere, anytime access, this is appealing to many people. This is because you need to pay the regular licensing fee along with the monthly subscription charges to use this feature. If you really want to access your data remotely in an affordable manner, then QuickBooks Online is the best program for you.

If you want a program that can be industry-specific, then QuickBooks Premier is the best option for you. It has a lot of features and tools that are well suited for various industries. They offer a lot of control options. This is why QuickBooks Premier is the best option for industries.

If you buy a lot of raw materials and manufacturing materials and want to keep and track inventory for the options, then QuickBooks Pro is the best option for you. If you think that this version is not able to handle your inventory properly, then it is recommended to go for a more advanced version of QuickBooks, such as the QuickBooks Premier.

If you have a small business and you do not need a lot of accounting features, then QuickBooks Pro is a good option for you. It can handle all the needs and requirements of a small firm. It is a great asset to accountants. If you want to use a small business program package, the QuickBooks Pro will really help you.

As said above, there are many different versions of QuickBooks with a variety of pros and cons. Just check what your business needs and choose the appropriate version accordingly.

Becoming a Certified QuickBooks ProAdvisor

There are many different bookkeeping programs available on the market. QuickBooks is one such program that is generally used by small businesses as well as other individuals as well.

Intuit, the parent company of QuickBooks, has a variety of programs to help you and fulfill all your accountancy and bookkeeping needs. One such program is QuickBooks ProAdvisor. This version allows you to hire accountants to help you. Similarly, you can get certified from Intuit using this version. The company generally certifies people who are proficient in using QuickBooks. They just need to take an exam to get this.

There are other certificates available from various firms such as NACPB or the National Association of Certified Public Bookkeepers that prove that you are proficient in QuickBooks.

Part 1

Preparing for the Certification Exam

Step One:

Before beginning the certification process, it is necessary to ask yourself why you need the certification. Many individuals can find the certificate unnecessary. It is true that you cannot claim that you have been certified by QuickBooks unless you take the exam and receive the certificate, but it does not mean that you cannot become proficient in the program without the certificate. You can master the software without the certificate with the help of training and self-learning. Another aspect of the certificate is that it is only related to QuickBooks. This means that the certificate does not help you with other accounting software that is available on the market. If your employers or clients think that you should be able to use other software along with QuickBooks, then this certificate will not help you in a significant way.

QuickBooks is just one of the many accounting programs available on the market. But what makes it one of the best ones is that it incorporates a lot of different accounting functions and options. But this does not mean that a QuickBooks certification can make you an accredited accountant. The certificate cannot make you a certified accountant or bookkeeper.

Step Two:

Intuit believes that it is necessary for people to have at least two years' experience before using QuickBooks for functions related to invoicing and payroll. Intuit also recommends having a two-year experience for creating cost reports and budgeting as well. But there exist no formal requirements or eligibility issues for the process of certification. A user can take the certification exam whenever he or she believes that he or she has the necessary skills and needs.

It should be noted that QuickBooks certificate is not necessary for business owners, bookkeepers, and people who are already experts in using the software. The certificate is necessary if you want to use the official logo and certification on your business accounts and resume. It thus serves as a marketing tool that can help you attract a lot of employees and customers as well. Nowadays, many employers seek people with QuickBooks expertise, so having a QuickBooks certificate can help you stand out from the crowd.

Step Three:

It is recommended to understand what is expected in the exam and what you should expect from the exam. Generally, the following skills will be put to the test in the exam:

- How to set up the software

- How to work with lists

- Using various bank accounts

- Input data in invoices and sales

- Using other QuickBooks accounts

- Entering as well as paying bills

- Receiving payments

- Making deposits

- Analyzing financial data

Step Four:

It is recommended to check out the variety of certificates that are available and choose one that perfectly fits with your needs and requirements. Intuit has different levels of training and certification. The certification is supposed to be a marketing tool that can be used to get better offers from employers and customers. So it is recommended to get a certificate that can help you target your 'target demographic.' Do not apply for random certificates if you believe that they will not help you. Instead, it is recommended to contact an expert and ask for his or her advice while choosing a certificate level. This will help you keep your journey towards certification effortless. Here is a list of various certification levels that are currently available:

ProAdvisor without Certification:

In this level, you get QuickBooks training material, but you do not receive any certificate. You will be able to learn all the basics of QuickBooks and understand some intricacies as well.

1. ProAdvisor with Certification in QuickBooks Pro/Premier: For this level, you need to take a simple test that will test you on many different functions of QuickBooks Premier and Pro. Passing this test will get you a certificate.

2. ProAdvisor with Certification in Intuit QuickBooks Enterprise Solutions: this level also involves a certification test, but this test is more complex than the one above. It is more focused on the QuickBooks Enterprise version.

3. ProAdvisor with Certification in QuickBooks Point of Sale: It is a complex test. This test and training are focused on the QuickBooks Point of Sale products.

4. Advanced Certified ProAdvisor: This is the most difficult test of all the tests. You need to take a complex test to get the certificate. In this test, you will also be tested for advanced functions of the program, troubleshooting problems, errors, using third party applications, job costing, and many other areas as well.

Step Five:

As said above, it is necessary to decide whether a training course and certificate are correct for you or not. If you are not confident about your current knowledge regarding QuickBooks, then it is recommended to join a QuickBooks training class. Here you can learn how to use QuickBooks efficiently, after which you can take the certification exam that you want and need. There are a variety of classes available now. Some of them are online, while a lot of them are offline as well. Some options include:

Official in-person or offline training is given by Intuit Academy. Many people think that taking a class devised by Intuit will help them become better than any other class, but this is just a myth. You can take classes anywhere; it does not matter.

1. An Authorized accounting firm: There are many different, authorized firms that offer various

training courses. They also offer certificate courses.

2. Bookkeeping class: It is also possible to classes on QuickBooks from various Bookkeeping institutes and classes. This is great if you want to learn QuickBooks but do not care about certification, as this method allows you to learn everything without taking the certification exam. It is necessary to check whether the class or institute is accredited or not. If the class is not accredited, avoid it.

Step Six:

Study Guides:

Another factor that can help you with the certification exam is getting a study guide. Nowadays, a lot of study guides are available on the market according to the level of difficulty. It should be noted that the certification exam is an open-book test. This is why getting a study guide is absolutely crucial as you can use it in the exam for references as well.

There are many different study guides available for QuickBooks. Many different websites offer free online tutorials, as well. These free tutorials can help you understand the difficult parts of the program.

There are also many paid versions of tutorials and study guides available on the market. Choose wisely.

Part 2

Taking the Certification Exam

Step One:

It is recommended to take as many practice exams as possible before taking the real exam. There are many practice exams available online that can help you to be prepared. You can find many practice tests by Intuit as well as other services as well. They are not necessary for the certification, but they can really help you to be well prepared. It is recommended to take at least two practice exams. The time for these practice exams is two hours, just like the official exam. As the official exam is an open book test, it is recommended to use your study guide while taking the practice exams as well.

Step Two:

To take the exam for QuickBooks certification, you need to sign up for it. The exam is overseen by the National Association of Certified Public Bookkeepers (NACPB). You are supposed to take the exam online with the ATTC or the Accountant Training and Testing Center.

Once you are ready to take the certification exam, just visit the ATTC website and click on the Schedule a Test page. Here you can choose the time and date on which you want to take the test. The ATTC will send you all the relevant details related to your exam on email.

It should be noted that while the test is offered by the official bookkeeping association, it is still related to QuickBooks only. It does not mean that you are a certified bookkeeper or an accountant. It only proves that you are proficient at QuickBooks.

The fee for the test is $150 if you are not a member of NACPB, but if you are a member of the NACPB, then you are supposed to pay $100 for the same.

If you fail the exam, you can retake the exam by paying a smaller fee. This fee is $50 for members of NACPB and $75 for nonmembers of NACPB.

Step Three:

The third step is obviously taking the exam itself. The exam has a fairly easy format. There are 50 MCQs or multiple-choice questions and simulations. To clear the exam successfully, you need to score at least 75%. This means that you need to solve at least 37 questions correctly. But don't worry, the exam is two hours long and is an open-book test. This means that you can consult with your book and check it while writing the test. Once you successfully clear the exam, you will receive an official certificate from the organization. You will also receive the certification logo, which you can use on your cards, banners, etc. This will help you attract potential employers as well as clients who want people proficient in QuickBooks.

As said above, even if you fail the exam, you can retake it for a discounted fee. It is recommended to stay up-to-date and keep your certificate up-to-date as well. You need to retake certain tests from time to time to keep your certificate up-to-date. This is necessary because QuickBooks changes a lot as the company keeps on introducing new features and functions. It is thus recommended to update your training and certificate every year. This will help you stay updated, relevant, and popular among employers. It will also help you attract a lot of clients who want an accountant who keeps himself or herself updated all the time.

CHAPTER EIGHT

QUICKBOOKS TIPS

Until now, we have seen the basics and important aspects of QuickBooks and how it can change your life. QuickBooks is surely one of the best business and bookkeeper software packages available on the market. It is well known for its variety of security features along with an elegant, sophisticated, and easy to use interface. It has a variety of features that make it the best software for accounting. It has multiple features, such as employee management, bank integration, etc. that make it highly popular and usable. While the learning curve of QuickBooks is not as steep as other software, beginners may still find it a bit difficult. It has many shortcuts and tips that can make your overall experience with the software easy. Even if you are an experienced user, it is possible that you may not know about all the secrets and tips that the software is hiding. This chapter will cover many different, useful, and crucial tips that will help you use QuickBooks in a far more efficient manner. Let us have a look at these tips one by one. These tips will surely help you become a master of QuickBooks.

Use ProAdvisor

This is a highly recommended tip for people who have just started using QuickBooks. ProAdvisor is a part of the Intuit Package. It is extremely useful as it allows you to connect with a local accountant. The accountant can help you with the software and other aspects as well. For instance, the accountant can also give you crucial advice on topics such as tax requirements and business structure. He or she can also teach you how to offset expenses. Thus, this option can help you prevent frustration and can help you save a lot of time as well.

Take Your Time to Understand the Basics

As said earlier, QuickBooks has learned, though not as steeply as other software. But this does not mean that an inexperienced or new user will find himself or herself at home right from the first use. You will surely need to spend some time to understand the basics of the software. One of the best ways to learn the basics of the software is by using the 'Getting Started Tutorials' options. In this option, you will learn how to manage bills, how to input costs, and various other aspects as well.

All the tutorials under the above option are extremely well made and well constructed. They are highly practical, as well. To avoid frustration later, it is recommended to invest a few hours on the tutorials in the beginning. These tutorials are sure to help you understand the basics of the software.

Passwords are Essential

Like your money, your financial data is crucial as well. Data theft has become a serious issue now. If you do not use a strong password, your hard-earned money may get stolen. It is necessary to choose a strong and difficult to guess the password to avoid any problems in the future. People generally connect their QuickBooks account with their bank accounts. If your QuickBooks gets hacked due to a weak password, the hacker will be able to access your bank details and accounts as well. Thus, to avoid any future problems, risks, and frustrations, it is recommended to choose a strong password. Never share your password, and do not write it down. Do not use passwords that can be guessed with ease. These include birthdays, anniversaries, phone numbers, etc.

If you cannot come up with a complex password, you can also use an online password creator.

Enter Correct Company Information

When you put the details regarding your firm into the software, do it correctly. Everything that you add to the software should be accurate. This includes your reporting forms, business structure, calendars, Tax ID number, etc. If you input the wrong data into the system, it may lead to serious problems later. It is recommended to enter all the correct details regarding your firm using the 'Company Tab.' It is always better to crosscheck the data before submitting it.

Input Accurate Customer Details

Like Company or Firm details, you should always enter the correct Customer details in your system. It is necessary to learn and understand the basics of how to set up a new customer in the system. To do this, just click on the Customers tab at the center of the screen and then input all the details. It is necessary to add to each customer as a new customer. It is also recommended to customize their payment options as a check, cash, or credit card.

If you are new to the world of QuickBooks, it is recommended to set up your core customers as soon as possible and then add new customers whenever they come. The user needs to be disciplined about this as it will help him or her to avoid further inconveniences. It will also make other tasks such as reconciliation and invoicing easy.

Inputting Employee Details

Many people use QuickBooks to pay their employees; if you are one of them, then it is recommended to understand the Employee related options carefully. QuickBooks can help you manage deductions, tax payments, benefits, etc. To utilize these features, just go to the Employees Tab. In this tab, you will find the Employees Center. Here you can set up employees in a quick and efficient manner. You can also view the reports in this section.

Reconciling on QuickBooks

While QuickBooks is already a great, efficient, and quick way to manage your books, you can make it even better with the help of constant reconciliation. It is necessary to reconcile your accounts regularly. This way, you will always have an idea of what is going on in your business. It is especially recommended to reconcile your accounts when you receive a statement or remittance. You should reconcile whenever you receive statements for loans, credit cards, bank accounts, etc.

Backing up QuickBooks

It is recommended to back up your data from time to time to keep it safe and secure. The best way to ensure that your data is being backed up or not is by setting an automatic schedule. Backing up your data needs to be one of your most important priorities. If you do not back up your QuickBooks (and if it is present on only one system), and the system crashes, you will lose your complete data.

Integrate your QuickBooks with your backup software to avoid data loss. You can also use the online version of QuickBooks. These versions back up your data directly to the Cloud. This way, you will never lose your data.

Print Checks Directly from QuickBooks

Printing check frequently is a highly time-consuming and expensive task. If you want to save a lot of time and money, you can print your checks using QuickBooks. Printing checks is easy; just click on the Banking Tab and click Write Check. Here click on Print. You will not have paycheck fees to your bank anymore.

Paying Bills via QuickBooks

Paying bills using QuickBooks is easy and timesaving. You can do this by using the Online Bill Payment Option. Using this method, you can avoid all unnecessary steps, and you can reconcile your accounts in no time. This will save you a lot of effort and time in the long term.

Customize Your QuickBooks' Layout

QuickBooks is extremely user-friendly. It allows users to change the interface and customize it according to their needs and desires. If you are accustomed to the old interface, you can change it back so easily. Just click on Edit, followed by Preferences, followed by Desktop View. Here you can change and customize the desktop according to your desire.

Customize Your Icon Bar

It is also possible to customize the Icon Bar in QuickBooks. Icon Bar is a timesaving option present in QuickBooks. Here you can put the link that you require and use the most. To customize your Icon bar, click on View, followed by Customize Icon Bar. Now customize the bar according to your usage.

Utilize Memorized Transactions

You can use QuickBooks to make your life simple. It allows you to make regular transactions automatically. To use this feature, just click on Lists, followed by Memorized Transaction List, followed by Memorized Transaction, followed by New Group. Here you can set up all the transactions that you want to be remembered. These can be used to send patterned monthly invoices or pay patterned bills.

Use Online Banking

QuickBooks can help you do online banking with ease. QuickBooks integrates online banking and makes it simple. To use Online Banking in QuickBooks, just click on the Online Banking option on the Icon Bar. A tutorial will begin. Once you finish the tutorial, you can start using online banking immediately. Be careful, though! It is recommended to pay close attention to your security. If more than one user utilizes the software, then it may lead to catastrophic results.

Setting Up 1099 Vendors

Many people use freelancers and contractors for help. Managing and keeping track of their transactions is a difficult problem that can be solved with ease using QuickBooks. It is possible to set up 1099 Vendors using QuickBooks. Using this option, you can sort your payments along with sales taxes to the independent freelancers. This will help you save a lot of time and frustration at the end of the year.

Turning Off Spellcheck

Spellcheck may seem to be a strange feature in QuickBooks, but many people find it useful and crucial. But if you are one of those people who do not like using this, you can shut it off. To turn spellcheck off, just click on Edit. Next, click on Preferences, followed by Speller.

Click on the box next to Always Check Spelling to turn the feature off.

Restricting User Access

If you believe that your software is being used by a lot of people and you think that it is a problem, then you can restrict user access as well. It is advisable to restrict user access because QuickBooks deals with a lot of intricate and sensitive data and functions. To restrict user access, the best way is to create multiple users and give them access to specific features only. This way, users can use the accounts for specific tasks only, and your personal data will remain safe.

Online Payments via QuickBooks

Another great feature of QuickBooks is that you can accept payments from the customers directly while simultaneously reducing the fees as well. To do this, you just need to enter and set up your bank details. These details can then be used by the customers to pay you directly. Each transaction only costs around 50 cents, which makes it a lucrative and highly affordable option. It is cheaper than many other options that are available on the market. Instead of considering these options and wasting your time, it is recommended to use QuickBooks simply.

Find the History of a Transaction

Finding invoices, memos, credit memos, payments, related invoices, and sorting them can be a time-consuming and difficult task. Managing these receipts and sorting them and storing them according to the records can take a lot of time. QuickBooks can help you save a lot of time by providing you a simple and elegant way to find the history of any transaction. Just click on the Reports option and then click on Transaction History. The history of all your transactions and related data will be displayed instantaneously.

Linking Your Email to QuickBooks

Nowadays, many people offer online services or have businesses that do not need any kind of physical invoices. In such businesses, it may become difficult to keep track of transactions. To solve this problem, just link your email account to QuickBooks. This way, you can send your invoices directly to the customer. You can also enable the option to receive email reports. You can link a variety of emails to your QuickBooks, including Gmail, Outlook, Yahoo, etc.

Viewing Double Entries

QuickBooks, like all other accounting systems, uses the Double Entry principle. This ensures its smooth functionality and adaptability. To check the double-entry of any transaction, just open the transaction and go to the Reports>Transaction Journal. This will help you to open a Transaction Journal. In this journal, you can check whether the double-entry has been posted properly or not.

Merging Similar Accounts

Sometimes, due to multiple accounts, a QuickBooks file may become too complex and heavy. This generally happens when different accounts are created by different employees for different tasks. This also happens when multiple customer accounts are created due to manual errors.

To make the process easy and manage the accounts efficiently, you can use the merging option. To merge, simply choose an account name and select the second account to merge it with. Right-click and paste the name of the account that you want to merge. Once done, click on save. This will successfully merge the accounts.

Chat with Staff

In QuickBooks, the staff has an option to use different accounts to chat using the QuickBooks window. Using this, your team can discuss entries and solve problems simultaneously. Using the chat option is easy. Just open the Company menu and click the Chat with a Coworker option. This will initiate a new chat.

Offset Invoices against Credit Notes

If you offset zero against credit notes, a lot of invoices may simply disappear. To avoid this, you should distribute credit notes against varied invoices. Due to this, only one invoice will not disappear.

Printing Batch Invoices

Sometimes a user may need to print many invoices together at one time. In such cases, it is recommended to utilize the Batch Printing option. To use this option, you just need to create invoices and then click the arrow near the Print option. Next, click on the Print Batch. This will present you with an option to choose the number of invoices to print. This will thus make the whole thing simple and timesaving.

CONCLUSION

Now that we have reached the end of this book, I am sure that by now, you must be well versed with the basics of QuickBooks. QuickBooks is an impeccable software that can help you with all your bookkeeping and accounting needs. This program is really great for people who want to make payments, generate invoices, generate customized reports, create lists for customers, lists of employees, lists of vendors, and export or import data from other applications as well.

As you have now understood the basics of QuickBooks, you can explore it and try to check out various other features of the program. QuickBooks comes with a lot of bells and whistles that make it a great bookkeeping program. It solely depends on you how you use the program.

One of the best things about QuickBooks is that it allows you to sync with the bank account and sync with debit as well as credit cards too. This allows you to stay up-to-date all the time. Whenever a new update comes up, you will stay functional. You can use your up-to-date knowledge to create budgets and keep your financial status healthy. There are many different features that are associated with QuickBooks. These features are good for experts as well as beginners.

The only thing that is left for users to do now is to understand and explore the variety of features and tools of this program. Try to check what features are suitable for you and which are not. You can also customize the program efficiently. You can also customize the lists, statements, etc. You can create lists that are customer-friendly and easy to understand, as well. It does not matter if you are not too familiar with the concepts of techniques and accounting. You can still use QuickBooks efficiently. You just need to check everything and take care of things. This way, you will avoid loss while learning new things. This software can really turn your business around if you know how to use it.

ACCOUNTING

A Beginner's Guide to Understanding
Financial & Managerial Accounting

By John Kent

INTRODUCTION

Accounting is one of those words that send shivers down the spine of even the most rugged individuals. When it comes to running a business, accounting is like the boogeyman that hides in the closet. It isn't that accounting is harmful, quite the opposite actually; accounting is a useful skill that should be part of your routine business. Many people start their businesses because of a passion, such as baking or carpentry. This passion fuels the desire to make a living through this manner and it is a delightful experience. Then accounting rears its head and the reality that running a business isn't simply fun and games sets in.

Accounting doesn't need to be this troublesome, though. There are numbers to be worked and this is intimidating to pretty much anyone who has ever sat through a high school math class. The truth is that accounting looks much harder than it actually is. It's one of those topics which becomes incredibly simple once you start to get your feet under you to form a solid understanding of how it is done. It still takes time and effort to ensure that you're not tossing away money through poor calculations, but this will come with time and there are accounting principles that are widely used and which help to make the process even easier.

With this book I aim to show you that accounting isn't as hard or as scary as you might have thought. We'll cover a lot of ground in a short amount of time but you'll be shocked at how little space you need for Accounting 101.

In chapter one, we are going to look at the importance of accounting. Why exactly is this skill so important? We're going to focus on accounting in businesses, rather than personal accounting. Some people will find that bringing this skill into their personal lives can improve their financial health but most people simply don't need it. However, we will briefly talk about tax accounting (and a few other types) in order to keep our eyes open to the ways we can continue to grow our accounting knowledge. Also important is the discussion we'll have on the difference between accounting and bookkeeping, two words which are often used interchangeably despite the fact that they aren't the same.

In chapter two we will lay down the basics of accounting. From the accounting equation to financial statements, we'll see what the main pieces of accounting are. This will be followed with a look at the principles of accounting in chapter three. These include acronyms like GAAP and IFRS, which seem far more complicated than they truly are when they're broken down into their letters this way. Once you shine some light on these, you'll realize that they're actually useful tools for making your life easier when it comes to your business's accounting process.

Chapter four will dive deep into financial statements. Get ready to learn all about the different statements you'll be using. These statements will help you to get a sense of where everything is and where everything is going, making sure that you have a clear and precise understanding of your financial situation. They really serve as the foundation for your financial decisions and you'll find that mastering them gives you a great advantage when planning what comes next for you and your company.

Chapter five will move into a discussion on the general ledger and how to proper record transactions. Without accurate accounting—i.e. updated and correct records—you can't make informed decisions. If you want to benefit from this skill set then you need to know how to record information effectively and without error. Again, this is an important process but one which is not nearly as difficult as you might think.

The last chapter will focus on managerial accounting. Managerial accounting deals with the internal aspects of the company. While financial reports and typical accounting must be done to a certain set of standards, managerial accounting stays inside the company and therefore it can use different metrics and standards to decide what is important. We'll look at how this form of accounting is used for goals such as forecasting and margin analysis.

By the time you finish this book, it is my hope that you will no longer see accounting as a monster in the closet but rather as one of the key tools at your disposal for ensuring that you spot financial problems before they are devastating. While it is always advisable to hire an accountant if you don't know what you're doing, it is important to take time and learn about these skills yourself. You may not want to take over your accounting duties yourself, even though it can be a way to save money, but a solid understanding will allow you to read and understand what you are being told so that you are never taken advantage of. To my mind, that alone is worth the price of admission for the book you hold in your hands.

CHAPTER ONE

IMPORTANCE OF ACCOUNTING

I can tell you that accounting is important but I'm sure that you've already heard this before. As soon as we start to look into launching our own business, no matter how small, we are buffeted with advice. Most of it simply stresses that you absolutely *have* to get an accountant. Or, depending on what part of the country you're in, you might hear "tax guy." Taxes are just another form of accounting and they typically mean it in a wider sense.

I am a firm believer that we don't follow advice in this manner. We can hear something a thousand times but never really get it. Instead of hearing what to do, it is important to hear why we do what we do. Once you understand the why behind accounting, all of the mystery dissipates and you see it in a new light. You might even see that it is easy to learn yourself if you're running a small enough business. The larger your business gets, the more the need for accounting increases, but so too does the size of the job. What takes a few hours for a smaller business takes up a lot more time once it's large. It is when accounting grows to this size that you are best served by hiring a professional for nothing else than letting you focus your attention on the problems that concern you the most.

In this chapter we're going to look at why accounting is so important for your business. With this grounding we'll then be able to look at the different forms of accounting there are such as financial, managerial, and tax accounting. There's other types too, but we'll cover those when we get there. We'll finish this chapter by clearing up an issue that confuses many people. Just what exactly is the difference between an accountant and a bookkeeper? Do you know? Or maybe they're the same thing? If you don't know the answer to these questions then don't worry, we'll sort all that out before heading on to chapter two.

Why is Accounting Important for Your Business?

There is a reason everyone has been telling you that you need an accountant. Accounting is one of the most important parts of keeping a business running. There are laws that have to be followed in regards to paperwork and money, otherwise you'll be running a criminal enterprise. That might sound a little bit extreme. I'm not saying you'll suddenly be part of the mafia or anything. However, your failure to follow regulations will lead to legal issues that will quickly shut down your business. If you don't run into this issue then chances are your lack of accounting led to financial issues that dropped the floor out from under your business.

The accountant's secret weapon is their ability to generate and analyse reports. Financial reports such as income statements, balance sheets, and cash flow statements all help to give you up-to-date financial information to understand exactly how well your business is doing. These statements cover things such as how much has been spent and how much has been earned by the company as a whole or over a set period of time. These might seem like simple documents and guess what? They are. But you're unlikely to use them until you understand how they are done and how to make the best use out of them.

As simple as accounting is when you first begin, you might think that keeping up on statements like these isn't very valuable. This tends to be an opinion that you see in much smaller businesses such as those with one to five employees, especially those that run online or don't require an office. These places have much lower overheads and so counting and following the numbers is much easier. The truth is that numbers, especially when it comes to finances, have a way of running away on us. It is just all too easy to overspend or lose track of where the numbers are supposed to be when you're keeping everything in your head. Study after study has shown us that we overvalue our memory's ability to retain information. By giving this information over to and running it through some basic accounting, you open your business up to a much greater range of tools and benefits.

One of the biggest benefits is that it reduces the chance that your business ends up on the wrong side of the law. Different states have different codes that must be followed in terms of what documentation you need to provide in order to run a legal business in the eyes of the IRS. There are tons of local laws that have to be followed about where you can open what business and what guidelines need to be followed for your industry and these may vary quite a bit, but you'll find that most states are closer together in terms of accounting regulations. You need to be aware of what liabilities you need to claim and, if you'll pardon the pun, be accountable for. These can be found with ease online for those looking to do their accounting themselves. An accountant for hire should be well-versed in local compliance already.

Beyond the legal side of things, it helps you to evaluate and operate your business from the most accurate perspective possible. By keeping accurate financial records you are able to manage your business much more effectively. Consider this on a small scale. You just work with your friend and you lend them the company credit card. When you get it back, they tell you they bought what was needed but forget to mention the can of pop they got. You're now working on slightly wrong information but if you jot it down and keep track then this can be sorted later. But what if you don't get back a price at all? Or what if you forget about that purchase on Thursday when it comes time to track everything next week? These are both arguments for why you need bookkeeping but this is going to have a direct impact on your accounting. In the short run you will find that your numbers are off and in turn this will cause you to be failing in your compliance because you appear to be misrepresenting your financial information.

Being off in the short term has profound effects on your accounting when it is used to its full extent. Accounting is most valuable when you use it to project forward to determine if the path you are on is working. By letting you forecast financial information to come, you can make plans on how to manage your business for success in the long term. Being able to make projections as to where you want to be and use these to build out a budget that will get you there, this is one of the most beneficial aspects to bring accounting into your life. If you have faulty information then you will make shoddy projections that fail to be reflected by reality. In a way, this is an argument for combining bookkeeping and accounting together as a skill set you want to learn rather than accounting alone, but it is a truly powerful tool for entrepreneurs to master.

Finally, don't forget that the financial statements you generate through accounting need to be filed with the appropriate authorities such as the Registrar of Companies. If your company is large enough to be on the stock exchange then this will mean even more paperwork to be done. Part of accounting is simply learning who needs to receive what paperwork and then generating it for them. This is probably the most important part of the process but it is also the least exciting. Once you learn how to tackle this, it is a piece of cake.

Accounting is important because it gives you valuable information and allows you to legally continue running your business. Really can't get away with running a business without a bit of accounting. Rather than spend a bunch of money to get someone else to do it, this book offers you the benefit of taking it into your own hands to keep your operating costs even lower!

The Big Two: Financial and Managerial Accounting

When it comes to accounting there are a lot of different types, but businesses are going to have two that pop up with a greater frequency. These are financial accounting and managerial accounting. These can be thought of as external and internal accounting. Financial accounting is the external one as it focuses on the financial information that is necessary for legal reasons. This is contrasted with managerial accounting which focuses on financial information for use within the company.

Financial Accounting: Financial accounting is the recording and grouping of financial information, such as transactions, into statements. These statements are used to provide information about your company's finances to people outside of the company. These could be creditors or banks looking to see if they should loan you money. This could also be to investors who are looking to get involved with your company. It is incredibly important that you keep records of this sort.

Financial accounting requires the use of a chart of accounts. This is a record of the financial transactions that your company has had and it is created in order to store financial information that can be used and referenced later on. There are certain rules and regulations in place in regards to how your chart of accounts and the information therein works. Financial statements that make their way into the accounts are released to the users of those accounts and lawsuits related to false financial statements are a common practice. It is extremely important that the information you use in financial accounting is always accurate.

One of the ways that this is achieved is by using an accounting framework such as the GAAP or the IFRS. We talk more about these in chapter three when we discuss accounting principles, but what is important to understand here is that these play a role in financial accounting and they help to shape the way that we create our statements. Whether or not you are a for-profit or a nonprofit organization will make a difference in which one you use and how you make your statements, but both nonprofits need to generate financial statements just as much as for-profits do.

As mentioned previously, those companies which are publicly-held and desire to sell shares through the stock exchange need to go through additional steps with their financial accounting. Publicly traded shares must comply with the regulations as set out by the Securities and Exchange Commission or SEC. This is an extra set of hoops that need to be jumped through but most companies aren't going to start out with shares to sell and so it is often only a concern for larger companies. However, their statements and compliance do fall into the realm of financial reporting and are worth keeping in mind going forward.

Managerial Accounting: Also known as management accounting, this form of accounting is focused entirely on the processing reports and data that will be used internally. This accounting covers the type of information that a manager needs to make informed decisions about daily operations, hence the name. Because it is used for internal use rather than external accountability, managerial accounting is more likely to be a little bit different everywhere you go. The information that is important for a particular company will be the focal point for reports and those that are less important to your company may be the most important to another. This results in a lot more variety in managerial accounting when compared to financial accounting.

One key point of managerial accounting is variance reports. This is the reporting on the difference between a projection and a measured result. This can happen on day-to-day cycles, weekly, monthly, or quarterly cycles. While it is an important element of managerial accounting it is far from the only thing it covers. Managerial accounting also deals with tracking and reporting on cash at hand, budgeting of capital funds, recording accurate inventory, ensuring that transfer pricing analyses and project profitability reports are generated. Pretty much any kind of report that can be useful for use within the company will find some reflection in managerial accounting.

You may learn a system of managerial accounting that works great for your company. Since it's internal, you don't need to follow any type of guideline when it comes to these reports. It is important, however, to keep in mind that internal and external accounting is completely different. You must follow guidelines when reporting outside of your company. Because you end up needing to follow guidelines no matter what, it can be a smart idea to try to keep your managerial accounting as close to the guidelines as possible. This simply helps to keep everything looking the same when it comes time to read the information and this has the effect of reducing possible errors.

Other Kinds of Accounting

I bet there are lots of people out there that didn't realize there was more to accounting than just the financial and managerial flavors. Accounting is one of those topics that everyone thinks they know and few actually do. There are actually a bunch of different types of accounting but they're not as important to us in our discussions throughout the book so we'll only look at them briefly here.

Cost Accounting: Cost accounting actually falls into the realm of managerial accounting but it is worth noting here, too. This form of accounting focuses on keeping track of the total cost of production a company has accrued through the assessing of fixed costs and variable costs.

Forensic Accounting: Forensic accounting is a field of accounting that seems a bit like a private investigator's job. In accounting you are mostly working from all the data and just putting it together in fascinating ways. In forensic accounting, you lack all of the necessary financial records you would need and so it is up to you to go through the available data to figure out what is missing.

This type of accounting is used by investigators to try to take down illegal businesses. By spotting financial records that are fraudulent, investigators can either press charges or gain insight into criminal operations in this manner. But forensic accounting isn't always used to catch crooks. Sometimes the reason that records are missing can be entirely innocent, such as when a business catches fire and loses some of or all of their records.

Most businesses won't ever hire a forensic accountant and if they do then it is likely that they are working on a freelance or a consulting basis. This is because forensic accountants aren't useful 99% of the time. When they are, they're one of the most useful people you could ever meet.

Governmental Accounting: This is a field of accounting that has a tight grip on the resources being accounted for. It also focuses on breaking down activities into different sections to make it crystal clear how the various resources involved are being used. However, it is unlikely that you will ever need to worry about government accounting for your business because it is pretty much exclusively used by the government, though the levels do differ. Local governments to the country-wide government all make use of this style.

Governmental bodies have their own specific needs when it comes to accounting. While we've briefly discussed the idea of accounting standards and how making them so widely accepted has helped reduce accounting errors, this whole conversation goes out the window when we discuss governmental accounting. This type of accounting uses entirely different standards from what your business or nonprofit uses. They go through the GASB or the Governmental Accounting Standards Board.

We could dive deep into governmental accounting and fill out the rest of this chapter but this would be meaningless to you. The important takeaway here is that the standards of governmental accounting are different from those you'll be using. If you want to learn more about governmental accounting then you are likely considering a job as a government accountant and you'll want to seek out more in-depth information and education.

Public Accounting: This is more a description of a business' services than a particular kind of accounting. Public accounting is the term used to describe a business that can be hired to provide accounting services. What this means exactly is going to be dependent on the situation at hand. A public accountant could be hired to look after your tax returns. In fact, this is the most common use of public accounting. But they could also be hired to help you prepare your financial statements for external use or they could help you audit your company or clients. Another extremely common service they are hired to provide is simple consulting services to help you understand how to integrate a new accounting system on your computers, or perhaps they are needed to help with some forensic accounting to find information that has gone missing.

A public accountant is going to have rules and restrictions surrounding what information they can use, what information they aren't allowed to see, and what services they can offer. One of the major restrictions which is encountered quite often is centered around auditing. There are a bunch of obstacles that must be overcome in order for a public accountant to be able to help with auditing, such as having to register their accounting company with the Public Company Accounting Oversight Board or PCAOB. This registration comes with annual fees and requirements in terms of paperwork that must be completed. These costs are simply too much for many smaller accounting firms to pay.

A public accounting firm can only truly run in an economically sound way by employing lots of certified public accountants. By having enough of them, they will be able to afford the licencing to perform audits. The certification for public accountants used to be directly related to their ability to perform an audit but it has since been expanded to be seen as a sign of a highly qualified accountant. This means that you can expect to pay more to a certified public accountant than an uncertified one. Many small businesses find that the cost of a public accountant is just too dang high.

Which is why I argue that you should learn these skills for yourself. That way you can save your money and put it into the projects that will benefit your business' growth the most.

Tax Accounting: We come, at last, to tax accounting. This is the one that most people understand, at least in a basic way. You need to follow rules and regulations for reporting the assets and liabilities from your business. It doesn't follow any of the accounting frameworks that we've previously mentioned but instead it replies on the Internal Revenue Code or IRC. A tax accountant uses the information you've provided them to generate the amount of taxable income you've had. Tax accounting is pretty complicated because the number on your financial records isn't necessarily the final number they're worried about. They have to look at assets, reporting rules, and all sorts of other information in order to come up with the final taxable number.

This can have a positive result or a negative one. I personally saw the power of a good tax accountant this year. When it came time to do my taxes, I did a quick job of them and handed them off to a friend of mine who does tax accounting for a living. With the numbers I had provided, I was expecting to pay about $500 in taxes when all was said and done. He took one look at them, shuffled things a little bit and made me $800 back from the government. I don't know how he did it, I still haven't had a chance to ask because he's been as busy as I am, but that is the power of a good tax accountant. While you can learn to do your taxes yourself, it can really be worth getting a professional's eyes on them when you are just starting out. Just make sure to ask lots of questions so you can understand what they've done to help you so you can use it for yourself later.

The Differences Between Bookkeeping and Accounting

Bookkeeping is the process of recording financial transactions and keeping track of everything. Accounting works off of this tracked information to analyze, report, summarize, and interpret what the numbers from bookkeeping tells us. Both of these skills need to be used together in order to have the best results but many people think they are the same thing. This is especially understandable in our current age where accounting software often doubles as bookkeeping softwares. We'll look more at the similarities in a moment. First, let's explore the differences between these two.

The first major difference comes in the form of the definition of each field. This may seem obvious but it can help us to get a better understanding. Bookkeeping is about the identifying and recording of transactions. Accounting is about the interpreting and communicating of this financial information. One way of thinking of this is that bookkeeping is the process of writing a book while accounting would be the process of reviewing that book. Or for another metaphor, bookkeeping is checking the supplies and preparing the recipe for supper while accounting is the act of putting all of the ingredients together. Both bookkeeping and accounting directly invoke each other but this invocation is not the same as an equivalence.

The next major difference is key. Bookkeeping is about the recording of data. This means that the information that bookkeeping focuses on is plain. There is nothing fancy about it in the least, there are no great discoveries waiting in it. Bookkeeping is in no way a skill that lends itself to making decisions. But the data from the bookkeeping can be given over to an accountant who will shape that data into all sorts of different reports and these reports are the single-most useful tool that a manager or CEO has at their disposal when making decisions about their business. Likewise, this shows that the objective of the bookkeeper is to, well, keep the books up to date. The accountant's goal is to make sense of the books to see what they tell about the direction the company is headed.

Bookkeeping does not require any special skills. In fact, if you have some paper and a pencil then you can start keeping your books easily. Simply jot down everything you spend and every dollar you make. You don't even need to worry about sorting them out or weighing them against each other yet. All of this comes from the accounting side of things where you need to understand what you are doing to properly fill out reports and financial statements. It is these statements which will help you to understand whether you're making money or losing money in the long term. Similarly, bookkeeping doesn't analyze the data it brings in. It doesn't place it into a report or a statement but nor does it really try any form of analyzing. It is all about the recording.

So there are the major differences between bookkeeping and accounting. For many years these differences represented quite a large gap between the two practices. A company would hire a bookkeeper and an accountant. For example, my father has worked as a bookkeeper for decades and when he first started out that was all he did. As technology has advanced, the need for bookkeeping has been met by software developers. Now the role of the bookkeeper and the accountant are much closer together than they ever were before and my father no longer finds himself working alongside accountants, but rather he is one these days. So while this section is to highlight the differences between these two, it would be a disservice not to see how these two are growing more similar all the time.

The Slow Merging of Bookkeeping and Accounting

As technology advances, the distinction between bookkeeping and accounting will continue to fade away. This is seen first in the way that software has taken over many of the functions of the bookkeeper. Likewise, some bookkeeping software has taken over some of the responsibilities of the accountant, such as being able to create financial statements. This makes sense when you consider that the accountant must work from the information the bookkeeper has provided. Accounting used to be done by hand, with accountants needing to remember how to do each and every part. Accounting software now takes care of the majority of the calculations based on what you input.

This has led to the decline of bookkeeping as a career because it is slowly becoming obsolete. You used to need a bookkeeper to look over all the various accounts and make sure that transactions were logged in each one accordingly. But, again, technology now manages a large portion of this. Programs like QuickBooks have revolutionized the business world by giving the tools for bookkeeping and accounting over to the everyman. Are you a freelancer? Then you can take care of all your bookkeeping and accounting needs by spending five dollars a month for QuickBooks self-employed service. A larger but still small company could easily find all their needs met by spending $15-$25 a month for the more advanced QuickBooks service.

You know what has really caused this merging obsolescence more than anything else? The invention of smartphones. Now everyone has the ability to keep a tiny computer in their pocket that can be loaded with all of the software they need to run their business, from logging employee hours to keeping track of the books and even generating reports. Everything you need can fit into your pocket. When you realize this is the case it becomes extremely hard to justify hiring an employee to take care of bookkeeping or accounting for you. It is only as your company grows that it starts to become more appealing.

Do you need a bookkeeper *and* an accountant? Not really. Most accountants looking for employment these days will include bookkeeping on their resume because they understand that technology has fused these two roles. They might be different from one another but that doesn't mean they need to be handled by different people. Throughout the remainder of this book, we're going to be speaking about accounting, but often we will be bringing in elements of bookkeeping because of how tightly related they are. This would likely make an old-school accountant (or bookkeeper) angry, but it is a reflection of the technological times we live in.

Chapter Summary

- Accounting is a wider field than many realize, with different types of accounting that can vary wildly from each other.

- Accounting is one of the most important aspects of running a business.

- There are laws that must be followed when it comes to accounting, otherwise your business will not be legal.

- Accountants generate financial statements which give a sense of where the company is currently but they can also be used to project into the future to estimate where the company is headed.

- Accounting takes the guessing out of your finances and lets you get solid numbers down in a form that you can play around with to test out different strategies before adapting them.

- Accounting isn't bookkeeping but many accounting programs now cover bookkeeping issues, too.

- The two big types of accounting that we are concerned with in this book are financial accounting and managerial accounting.

- Financial accounting is concerned with recording and grouping financial information into statements. These statements are useful for investors to get a sense of how your company is doing and where it is spending its money.

- The financial statements that we generate in financial accounting are required by law and it is extremely important to ensure that the information in them is accurate.

- Information is kept accurate and easy to read by the use of an accounting framework like GAAP or IFRS, depending on where your business is located.

- Companies that are publicly traded have more paperwork to fill out in their financial accounting than those that aren't.

- Managerial accounting is a type of accounting that processes reports and financial data for use within the organization. Because managerial accounting is undertaken for internal use only, there is no specific accounting framework that must be used.

- Managerial accounting makes good use of variance reports, reports that show the difference between a projection and a measured result. This helps to give a sense of how the company is performing compared to how it was expected to perform.

- While financial accounting and managerial accounting are the two most important for beginners to learn, there are all sorts of other types of accounting, too.

- Cost accounting is a form of accounting that keeps tracks of the total cost of production that a company has built up.

- Forensic accounting is a fascinating field of accounting that combines accounting with detective work. Forensic accountants recreate books and records using partial or obscured data. Many work in some form of investigative capacity but others specialize in recovery such as when financial records are lost to technical error or in an accident like a fire.

- Governmental accounting is a form of accounting that is used exclusively by the government and it can have quite a variety of unique rules to it based on location. Most businesses will never have to worry about governmental accounting.

- Public accounting is more a name for a service rather than a style of accounting. If a firm hires accountants out to the public or to other businesses then these accountants would be considered to work in public accounting. Ever since 2002 there have been more rules than ever about what a public accountant can and can't do and there is lots of paperwork that a public accountant must have in order to legally work in the field.

- Because public accounting can be such an expensive career path, it is unlikely that you will encounter small-scale public accounting firms. It makes more sense economically for these firms to function at a larger-scale.

- Tax accounting is the form of accounting that learns tax law. A good tax accountant can save you lots of money by knowing how to properly claim expenses and juggle numbers.

- Bookkeeping is primarily concerned with keeping track of the accounts and logging all the necessary transactions. Accounting is concerned with generating financial statements and making projections about the future of the company.

- Accounting and bookkeeping go hand-in-hand, with bookkeeping being necessary for the accounting department to work their magic. Small companies will find that they can combine these two jobs together to save money.

In the next chapter you will learn the definitions behind some of the most important accounting terms. We'll cover all of the basics from assets to liabilities and from financial statements to the accounting equation. These basic concepts will crop up again and again throughout the book so it is important that we cover them in-depth before we get too much further.

CHAPTER TWO

ACCOUNTING BASICS

How much do you know about accounting already? Can you describe the accounting equation? Can you define the difference between your company's assets and liabilities? What about a financial statement? We've mentioned them quite a few times already throughout the book but do you really understand what we mean by them?

In this chapter we're going to work our way through these questions and more. This chapter can be considered almost like a glossary for the discussion to come. Without tackling these questions we won't be able to continue forward on the same page. And if there is one thing that I want us to share, it is the page that we are on. So if you were able to answer all of the questions in the previous paragraph then this chapter isn't going to cover anything you don't yet know, but if you struggled with even one of them then you'll want to stick around.

What is the Accounting Equation?

The accounting equation is a bit of an intimidating name. Yes, it does mean that there will be math to tackle. Though this shouldn't come as a surprise considering that we're discussing financial information, after all. The accounting equation is basically the foundation of any double-entry accounting setup. You see the accounting equation on your balance sheet where it is used to weigh your assets against your liabilities and shareholders' equity.

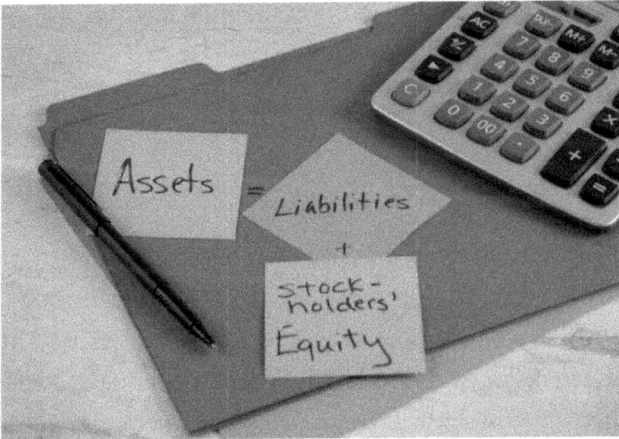

The accounting equation's formula is quite simple:

Assets = Liabilities + Owner's Equity

To calculate the accounting equation you need to find all of your company's assets on the balance sheet for the period you're looking at. Next you must add up all of the liabilities that the company has. The liabilities should have their own listing on the balance sheet. The third step is to locate the total of the shareholders' equity and combine this to the total from your liabilities. This finally gives you the last number, as combining the total from liabilities to the total from shareholders' equity will give you the total assets you have.

This simple equation is the cornerstone of accounting. You need to understand assets, liabilities, and stockholders' equity to get a full picture of the importance of this equation.

What are Assets?

An asset is anything that you own that has a value or that can be converted into money. Every company has its own assets but so does every individual. Assets are often used in order to create a cash flow at a later date, such as when you purchase a patent or a piece of equipment that you need in order to run your projects. For example, a lawn mower is a piece of equipment that counts as an asset. You could always sell it if you need to but it will make you cash down the road when you start to use it to mow lawns for your clients.

Personal assets are typically valued either at the individual level or at the household level for families. These include cash and cash equivalents and this can include the cash you have on hand and as well as the cash in your bank account. Any property you own counts as an asset and if you have a house or other building on that land then this also counts as an asset. Certain personal possessions count, such as vehicles, boats, furniture, jewelry, collectibles, and more. However, it is this category of assets that makes for the most confusing calculation as there are strict laws around which items can and cannot be counted as assets. Less difficult to understand is that your investments, all of them from mutual funds to bonds and retirement plans, count as assets. All of these assets are combined to give you a number. This number has your liabilities subtracted from it in order to give you what is called your net worth.

A business asset is anything of value that your business owns rather than you yourself. If you drive your car to work then that car is a personal asset but if you have a company car then that would be an asset of the company and not one of yours. Business assets can include machinery like this, as well as property, the raw materials used for making your goods, and those goods that you have in inventory already. These are all tangible assets.

Intangible assets are things such as any intellectual property your company owns, the royalties they receive from previous projects, and any patents you have registered. The balance sheet will show all of your company's assets, as well as whether they have been paid for already or whether they are under debt.

Assets are further broken down into current assets and fixed assets. A current asset is one that you can turn into cash within a year. Cash is a current asset, since you don't need to turn it into anything to begin, but so too are cash equivalents like treasury bills or bonds. Marketable securities, accounts receivables, and your inventory are all considered to be current assets. Fixed assets are those which are used in the production of goods or in the process of the services you offer. These are things like vehicles, machinery, buildings, land, furniture, and the like. These items could technically be converted into cash at a short notice if need be but they aren't accounted for in this manner. For example, you could sell a building in a week if you were lucky but you can't guarantee that you can achieve this so it is a fixed asset rather than a current one.

In order to fully appreciate assets, you need to remember that liabilities interact with them such as when your net worth is calculated by taking your liabilities out of assets. To see why liabilities are subtracting from your personal assets to make your net worth but are added with owner's equity to equal a company's assets, you're just going to have to keep reading.

What Are Liabilities?

Liabilities are one of the places that people begin to get confused when it comes to accounting. Assets are pretty easy to understand as they are basically possessions. Whether you possess something or your company does, the owner of that possession can view it as an asset. It doesn't cover items with sentimental value such as a seashell you were gifted by a loved one, so not every possession is an asset, but most people don't have any trouble with wrapping their head around this one.

Liabilities are different. Liabilities are what you owe. They tend to be dealt with over time rather than straight away. Liabilities can be settled by exchanging money, goods, or services. If I write a book for a company that is going to pay me at a later date then this promise of pay is a liability (though it must be noted in a legal fashion, otherwise there is not a real liability but rather an informal one). Liabilities as noted on the balance sheet include things like loans and mortgages, premiums, and deferred revenues. Because they deal with something that isn't really solid but more like a conceptual category of information, it can be quite difficult to sort it all out. This is made even more confusing when you take into account that your liability can change when you get married or start having children.

The most common liability is a financial liability. If you hired a consultant and have received their bill but haven't paid it yet then this becomes a financial liability. You are liable for the amount you owe. Basically, a liability is an obligation to settle at a later date. The later date part is important. If you paid your gardener in cash for their services then this is a cost, not a liability. But if they gave you their bill on Friday and you plan to pay it on Sunday then you have a liability for those two days. This is a very, very short-term liability. Most liabilities that accrue through your business will be divided into short-term or long-term liabilities. Short-term liabilities are those that should be cleared in less than a year and long-term liabilities are those that are expected to take a year or more.

Liabilities are common in pretty much every business. If you are running a store then you will be dealing in cash transactions with your customers and so it is unlikely that liabilities will arise from there. But you are likely to be liable to manufacturers and suppliers you work with to get your raw materials. It is in this part of your business that the liabilities really pop up. If you aren't running a store but are providing your goods to other stores to be sold then chances are you are the one who will be expecting a pay and so you'll be the only handing out liabilities.

So liabilities are promises to pay. When you are calculating your own net worth, you don't calculate what you still owe. Your business must take this into account in the accounting equation or it will result in misrepresented financial information that can cause legal issues you'd rather avoid.

What is Stockholders' Equity?

Stockholders' equity is the phrase we use to refer to the assets that a company has available for shareholders once all of the company's liabilities are paid for. A stockholder is of course any individual that owns one or more shares in a company's capital stock, these shares are primarily common stock for most companies within the United States. Stockholders are separate from a company and thus they are considered to have limited liability in regards to the company. Common stockholders will help to elect a corporation's board of directors and they typically vote on issues such as mergers.

A company's stockholders' equity is typically calculated by totalling all of the company's assets and subtracting its liabilities. Another form of calculating a company's stockholders' equity is by totaling the share capital and retained earnings and subtracting any treasury shares, which is the term used to describe stock that a company has purchased back from shareholders. Stockholders' equity can be used as a way of viewing a company's success. If a company has a positive stockholders' equity then that company is doing well, or at least managing to get by. When a company has a negative stockholders' equity then we are often right to guess that the company will be declaring bankruptcy or folding in the near future.

Stockholders' equity begins with the money that is invested in the beginning through those that purchase shares. This is then combined with the retained earnings the company has managed to acquire through their operations. The initial investment is extremely important in the beginning, as that is where most of the money to launch the business comes from. The longer a business has been functioning, the less important this initial investment becomes while the retained earnings continue to grow. Basically, stockholders purchase into your company with the expectation that the business will make money. Retained earnings are expected to grow, thus making back the initial investment that is represented by purchasing shares.

As a company continues to grow, they often end up engaging in share buybacks to create treasury shares. Everyone that has a share in the company is entitled to a portion of the company's earnings, typically in what is called a dividend. Since every stockholder represents more money leaving the company each quarter in dividend payments, it is often beneficial for a company with large retained earnings to purchase back shares by buying out a stockholders' shares. This process of buying back shares creates treasury shares and, while these still count towards a company's total issued shares, treasury shares do not count as outstanding. This means that the company does not need to take these shares into account when paying their quarterly dividends or when they are calculating the earnings per share. Treasury shares can always be sold at a later date when the company has a need for raising further capital or they can be retired to no longer have any value.

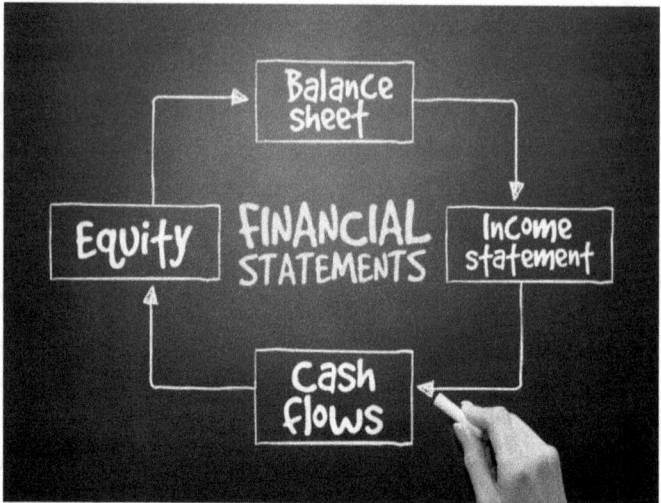

What Are Financial Statements?

Financial statements are simply written and logged records that each company is required to have in order to show what activities they have been taking part in and how those activities have performed financially. Financial statements are neutral documents which convey information on the reality of a company's financials and therefore they are quite boring as there is no spinning of the numbers or creating a narrative of the company's progress. They represent a company when it has been boiled down to the purely numerical.

Financial statements are extremely important as various governmental bodies require them to be provided by scheduled dates and they can be audited at any time.

Audits are one of those terms that everyone understands to be bad but they really aren't. An audit is simply the process whereby an authority or someone acting on behalf of an authority performs an official inspection of your company's accounts. Audits are most often performed by someone working independently of your company, unless of course we are talking about an internal audit in which case the information is less official and more important for making informed decisions and catching errors before financial reporting. Audits are often performed by the government in order to ensure that you are being honest to investors and paying the appropriate taxes.

Financial statements are used to judge how well a company is performing and to make informed estimates regarding how the company will grow financially in the future. Financial statements come in several forms such as balance sheets, cash flow statements, and income statements. It must be noted here that financial statements aren't the end-all be-all documents that many seem to think they are. While they are neutral documents, there is room to interpret the data therein in different ways and it isn't uncommon for one investor to read a financial statement and arrive at a completely different opinion on the company's success when compared to another investor. This flexibility of interpretation may be seen as a positive in the realm of something like literature and narrative but it is a limitation in regards to financial performance and it is often best to provide investors with more information through additional documents, like road maps that show which direction the company is headed.

As financial statements are such an integral part of accounting we will be looking at them in-depth in chapter four where we will speak at length about balance sheets, cash flow statements, income statements, and statements of retained earnings.

What Are Taxes?

Taxes are one of those things about life that we can't escape from, like breathing or dying. Okay, maybe they aren't quite as bad as that last one, but there's more than enough sayings equating the two. Taxes are fees that the government levies on both individuals and businesses. By collecting taxes the government is then able to fund things like schools, hospitals, and the military, as well as smaller services such as roadwork.

Taxes come in many different forms. Income tax is placed on the money that an individual makes. Corporate taxes are collected from businesses. Sales tax is collected on many different goods at the point of sale. Property taxes are calculated and paid based on how much an owned piece of land and property is worth. Tariffs are taxes which are paid when importing goods and estate tax is calculated based on the value of a person's estate at the point of their death. We aren't going to be concerning ourselves too much with taxes throughout the book and this is the only point that we'll be mentioning many of these.

It is worth understanding corporate tax a little bit better, though. This tax is placed on the profit that your company makes, otherwise known as operating earnings. This is calculated by deducting expenses. The tax rate, as set by the government, is applied to the operating earnings to arrive at the amount your company owes in taxes. Because expenses are deducted before taxes are calculated there are some tricks that businesses use to reduce the amount of tax they need to pay. One well known example comes from Hollywood where film companies would purposefully make a movie that they knew was going to tank at the box office. If the movie made money for them then it would increase their earnings and thus increase the size of their taxes. But if they lose money on the movie then that was an expense that brings down their operating earnings so that they can land in a less expense tax bracket.

I do not recommend that newer companies try to play the system to this degree. It is likely to end you up in trouble, as the younger a company is the easier it is for expenses to get out of hand. Do keep in mind that the more you earn, the more you must pay. Sometimes it is best to push a profitable project a few weeks or even months down the road so that the profits aren't in yet when it comes time to calculate your taxes.

Chapter Summary

- The accounting equation is the foundation of any double-entry accounting system.

- The accounting equation is: **Assets = Liabilities + Owner's Equity**.

- We need to figure out what assets, liabilities, and owner's equity is in order to understand this equation. Each of these components makes up the basic building blocks of accounting.

- Assets are anything of value that can be turned into money. They can be used to create cash flow at a later date and include things from the company's actual on-hand cash to equipment that allows you to generate income at a later date.

- Personal assets are something that every individual owns and they can be looked at both on a personal level as well as on the level of a family for those who are married or have children.

- Personal assets include vehicles, boats, furniture, jewelry, collectibles, and more. They also include investments, mutual funds, bonds, and retirement plans. All of these assets are combined together, at which point your liabilities are subtracted, and you end up at your net worth.

- A business' assets are items that have been bought by the business rather than by any of its employees. A work car, equipment for production, the property and raw materials for the store, any stock already in inventory, all of these are examples of the assets a business owns.

- Tangible assets are like those we just mentioned but intangible assets include items like any intellectual property the company owns or any royalties it receives.

- Assets are divided into current assets and fixed assets.

- Current assets are assets which can be turned into cash within a year.

- Fixed assets are any assets that take longer than a year to turn into cash such as property.

- Liabilities are what you owe and they are typically dealt with over time by paying them back slowly. However, they typically increase before expansions as you raise or borrow more money in order to grow the company. While everyone dreams of paying off all that they owe, it is very common for successful companies to never end up paying off all their liabilities at the same time.

- When you perform a service for someone and hand them their bill with a date for a later payment then they are liable to you for that money. These do not count as our liabilities when doing accounting for our company but rather a way to see how liabilities are gathered.

- Even stores that deal primarily in cash are likely to end up with some liabilities on their hands when dealing with manufacturers and supplies. They have a way of stacking up even when you don't expect them to.

- Stockholders' equity are the assets that a company has available after all the company's liabilities have been paid off. This doesn't mean that the liabilities themselves have been paid off but rather that we have added up all of our liabilities and then removed that much of our revenue to get the amount we have in stockholders' equity.

- A stockholder is any individual that has purchased shares in your company. This is most often done so that the stockholder can earn a dividend, a regular payment of part of the company's finances. The size of the dividend a person receives depends on how many shares they own and how much each share is worth.

- A company may have treasury shares. These are shares that they have purchased back from shareholders to keep for themselves. Treasury shares still count as issued shares but they don't require the company to pay any dividends.

- A company with a positive stockholders' equity is doing well while one with a negative stockholders' equity is probably going to fold in the near future.

- A company's retained earnings are added to the stockholders' equity and so it often begins with money from investors but it should continue to grow beyond investors through money retained from earnings.

- Financial statements are statements which convey information and hard data about a company's finances for a given period of time. They are neutral documents that give investors and government workers the ability to see your company's financial records without any obscuration.

- Financial statements are made following a set of standards which helps to keep everything looking the same for ease of reading.

- Financial statements must be kept and they must be honest. There are many laws surrounding what you cannot do with your financial statements and punishments are higher now than ever before.

- Taxes are fees that the government places on both individuals and businesses. There are all sorts of different taxes and how much a company pays depends on how the company does, how much it spends doing that and how much it earns.

- Taxes are used to improve the infrastructure of the county and to fund public works.

In the next chapter you will learn about the different frameworks that we use in order to keep our financial reports in legal order. These include the Generally Accepted Accounting Principles or the GAAP and the International Financial Reporting Standards or IFRS. Which of these you need to follow depends on whether you are running a nonprofit or a for-profit organization but both types of businesses need to follow these standards in order to ensure they are compliant, which is a whole new can of worms that we'll get into next.

CHAPTER THREE

ACCOUNTING PRINCIPLES

Now that we have an understanding of the basics it is time to turn our attention towards the principles of accounting. These range from the frameworks we use, such as GAAP or IFRS, to ideals such as the revenue recognition principle, the historical cost principle, the matching principle, the full disclosure principle, and the objectivity principle. As you'll see, a good framework covers these principles.

We will begin with these principles then move into our frameworks. This will have the effect of showing us what "good accounting" is and how we achieve it through either GAAP or IFRS. We'll compare GAAP and IFRS against each other to see how they are similar, how they differ, and what you need to know about using them. Finally, we'll close the chapter on a discussion of compliance within accounting.

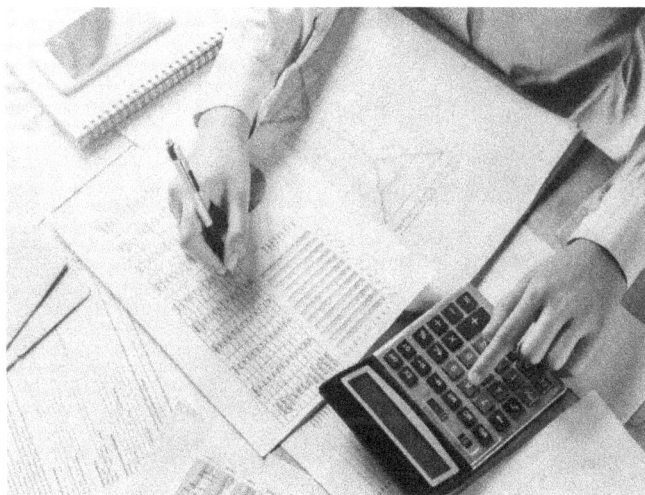

The Principles of Accounting

If you are going to run a business and keep everything legal and above the books then you absolutely must learn these principles and keep them in mind when doing your own accounting. A professional accountant will already know these and follow them closely, so you don't need to worry about a professional you hire messing them up. When you are learning to be your own accountant it is extremely easy to overlook these principles and end up causing errors and headaches down the road.

Never forget that the core of accounting, even more so than finances, is accurate and replicable reporting. I want to recommend that those learning accounting for the first time take extra caution when starting out. Don't just generate a single statement and call it a day. Go through the numbers a second time and generate the report again to make sure that the outcome is the same. This is not a principle of accounting that we'll be looking at but rather a principle for those beginning accounting.

So with that said let us dive into the key principles.

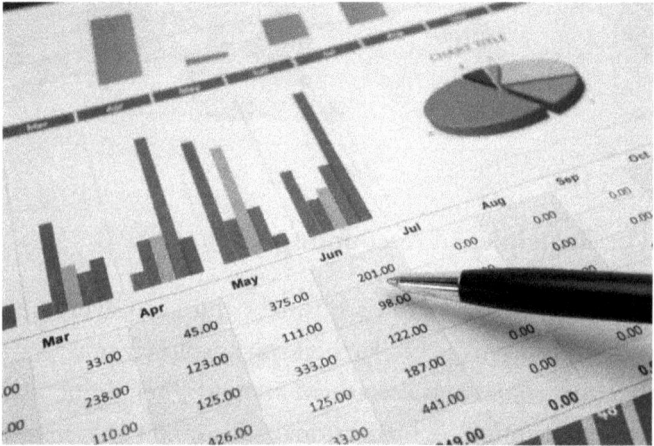

Revenue Recognition Principle: This principle is incredibly important, seems like common sense, and yet is often one of the those broken the most often. The revenue recognition principle informs us that we must recognize revenue as income. If you are running a coffee shop and you hand a customer their cup, the money they hand you is revenue. Revenue can come from selling goods or performing services. It can also come from sources like royalties or dividends.

For the most part you shouldn't have much trouble with understanding this principle. The hardest part of it comes from realizing just how easy it can be to break it. To use a personal example, I have a friend that runs a tattoo shop for a living who was training a new artist. As a new artist, he wasn't earning an income through the shop yet but rather they were training him at a loss with plans for future profits. He had to find his own clients and he couldn't charge them but he was getting hands-on training from professionals with thirty-plus years of experience. However, he had to be let go because he broke the revenue recognition principle and he opened the business up to a threat.

How did he do this? He took a $50 tip after a session. You might think that a tip isn't part of the business's revenue but it absolutely is. By taking the money and not informing the company, he unintentionally shoved them into illegal waters. There was no purchase and the service itself was free but by not reporting that tip the young artist broke the first principle of accounting. So it is important to keep your mind broad when you are considering revenue. It is always best to keep track of every single cent that comes into your company when it does, you can always remove them from your reporting later if it turns out that they are unnecessary.

Historical Cost Principle: This principle is applied to assets which a company has purchased at a cost. There are some assets which a company can acquire without paying anything. For example, pretend a well-known celebrity tweeted their praise of your services. This is great for marketing, it is fantastic for bringing in new customers, it is an asset. But it is not an asset in the way that accounting views assets and so it is irrelevant. Assets which cost money are important because they play directly into the historical cost principle.

When you purchase assets you must record the price they were purchased at. It is this price that will be used in your accounting. If the price changes (both higher or lower), it doesn't matter. You purchased the asset at the price you have recorded and it is this price that you will use for your accounting going forward. If you purchase additional assets at a different price then they must be recorded but the newly recorded price is carried forward.

This principle is important for keeping track of your finances. Say that one of your assets is a piece of technology that you purchased brand new. A few years later and the company is no longer producing that particular model. Collectors are now purchasing them at an inflated price. Even if the average price is now ten times as much as it was when you bought it, you have to list it at the original price. This helps to keep your records in order but it can also be beneficial, as the company could now sell this asset and earn a much greater profit compared to what they were valued at holding onto the asset.

Matching Principle: The matching principle can be a harder one to understand. It took me a little while to wrap my head around it at first. The principle itself is quite simple, however, once you sort it out. What the matching principle is all about is making sure that your expenses are accounted for during the same period of time that the revenue they're connected to is claimed. This can be a little confusing because what if you purchased supplies months ago and just used them to sell something today? Would that earlier expense not be applied until now?

Actually, yes, but there's more to it. It is easier to consider this principle with an example. Let's say that your employees are paid once a month on a set day. On the 10th of every month, your employees are paid out the earnings that they have acquired through sales commissions or similar. If your employees make 10% commission and they have sold $50000 in the accounting period, they would be paid their 10% commission in the following month, outside of the accounting period in question. However, the income that expense comes out of is accounted for in the given month and this means so to must that payment. So while you haven't technically paid your employees that $5000 yet, you do need to count it in the same period because the income the expense is related to needs to be recorded.

This principle disregards the timing of payment and it disregards your real cash flow. That $5000 did not leave the company during this time period after all. What it does is narrow the focus onto the accrual of expenses and revenue from the period.

Keep in mind that the matching principle does not mean that every expense needs to be matched. There are expenses like rent that aren't related to your revenue and therefore there is nothing to match it to. Income itself has to be matched to expenses.

Also keep in mind that this needs to be compared against your inventory, too. If you sell 100 units of your most popular item then you would have to record the cost of goods for 100 units. But if in that same period you purchased 10 more units then your real cost of goods sold is 90 units. So making sure that your expenses for goods sold is a matter of balancing expenses, revenue, and inventory.

Full Disclosure Principle: Out of all the principles in this chapter, this is the one that is the easiest to explain. What the full disclosure principle tells us is that the financial statements we generate must be about conveying information to the reader. As the readers are going to most likely be either in the government or they're going to be your investors, it just makes sense to convey information to them. What is important here is that you also aren't using your financial statements to conceal information. This would be money laundering.

In order to achieve this principle, all you need to do is tell the truth. Do your best to follow the principles that we have been discussing and do your best to keep all of your records honest. Issues may come up in which you accidentally mess up on a financial statement. This can be a real pain but catching it and owning up to it will still let you follow this one. You might break it in the short term on accident but you show that you want to fix it and ensure that your company is run with full disclosure.

One of the ways that accountants have improved their accountability to offer an even fuller disclosure is to present their financial statements alongside notes. While it is not required, you are always more than welcome to append a note onto your statements. This can help you to explain what happened in the period and what those reading the statements are seeing. Just remember that these notes are meant to be used to increase your disclosure and thus your honesty. You could append notes and fill them full of lies to hide the truth but this would be illegal, immoral, and it would absolutely be concealing financial information and thus breaking the full disclosure principle.

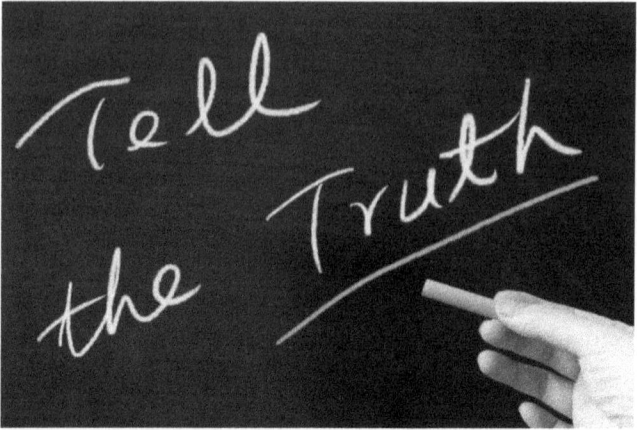

Objectivity Principle: The final principle that we'll look at before digging into GAAP and IFRS is the objectivity principle. This one is tightly tied to the full disclosure principle in that it is focused on keeping you as honest as you can be. In the full disclosure principle, that honesty is achieved by ensuring that all the relevant financial information is in place and accounted for. The objectivity principle relates less to the amount of information present and instead it looks towards the presentation of the data.

Financial statements are used in order to help project into the future. They give a sense of where the company is now and where they are going. But, as mentioned before, they have a limitation: they aren't concrete. Rather, financial statements can reveal different information to each person that reads them depending on what framework they want to view the information from. Because each person has their own bias as to what is or isn't a good sign, it can be easy to look at the data with our own perspective and want to make it reflect that. However, this would not be objective reporting but rather it would be subjective reporting and that has no place in the world of accounting.

By keeping the objectivity principle in mind we remember that the financial data we are reporting on must remain free from any personal bias. It must remain objective, not subjective. To do this we have to make sure that the data we use is verifiable. If we cannot verify where a number has come from then we have no use for it. Transactions need to have receipts and invoices and whatever documentation is necessary to prove it exists in a court of law. Of course you aren't going to need to go into a court of law if you are objective and commit to full disclosure, but you want to ensure that your financial statements are solid enough that they'd win any case.

If they aren't objective, they aren't solid.

What is GAAP?

GAAP stands for Generally Accepted Accounting Principles. And guess what? You've just learned about the biggies. These standards are widely used, you might even say that they are generally used. Having seen the principles themselves, you should be able to understand why they are maintained. For example, telling the truth and making sure that everything can be tied to documentation is just smart.

Others, such as the matching principle, are a little bit more elusive. It's not that the matching principle really represents the best option for handling numbers. It's possible that it is but what matters is not whether or not it is the best but rather that it is the most generally used. This is where the GAAP really benefits accountants. If you are an accountant that has been hired to take over for a company then it is a lot easier to settle into the position since everything is laid out how it should be. In a way, using something besides the GAAP would be akin to doing your accounting in another language.

We covered the key principles but I would recommend reading the Federal Accounting Standards Advisory Board's handbook on accounting standards. The PDF is available for free online at fasab.gov/accounting-standards. There is a lot of information in their handbook and much of it will be irrelevant to you. It would be unrealistic for a beginner in accounting to read the whole book. It is better to instead use your electronic search tools to find those sections dealing with the topics your company handles.

The GAAP has many topics that fall under its purview, too. These cover assets, derivatives, equity, expenses, the presentation of your financial statements, foreign currency, fair value, revenue, leases, hedging, and more. This wide range of topics means it is best to assume that a particular item is discussed in the standards. It might not be, but if you assume that it is and quickly search the document, you will find that this is the safer approach while you are still figuring out which elements apply to your situation.

The GAAP is not the only standards guide when it comes to accounting. There is also the IFRS, so let's take a quick look at that.

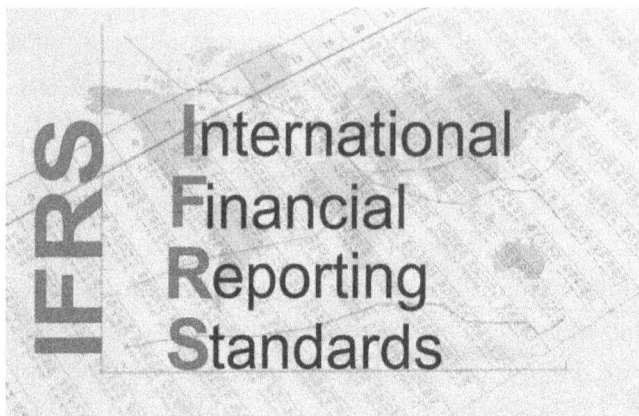

What is IFRS?

The answer to that question is the International Financial Reporting Standards. These standards are looser than the standards of the GAAP. They're also used in most countries. They deal more with the principles around accounting rather than with rules. There are a lot of rules in the GAAP, which is why it is good to become familiar with the search feature when dealing with them. This results in the IFRS being much easier to deal with.

GAAP vs. IFRS

The GAAP has been around longer and this means it is a much more comprehensive and complete set of standards in comparison. However, the GAAP is mostly used in the US while the IFRS is used around the world. If you are in the US then you should worry about following the rules as laid out in the GAAP. If you are located anywhere else then you will want to familiarize yourself more with the IFRS but keep in mind that you still might have to learn the GAAP.

IFRS approaches standardization of financial reporting through a system of standards. This means that it follows principles rather than rules. The principles we looked at in the first half of this chapter are important enough to set up the concept for what we are trying to achieve when reporting but there are many more rules in the GAAP.

While the International Accounting Standards Board doesn't actually make the GAAP, they are extremely influential in the way that it forms. They have no legal power over it whatsoever but when they put new standards they tend to be worked into multiple countries' standards. The new standard might go through a process of interpretation in which it may change or be slightly altered in order to be adapted. This in turn leads to the new standard helping to alter what a particular country's generally accepted accounting principles are.

But in the US, IFRS is irrelevant. The American GAAP are set by the Financial Accounting Standards Board and that's that. There have been movements for the US to switch to IFRS and the Securities and Exchange Commission have looked into it on certain occasions but they repeatedly turn down the concept. So for the time being, those in the US need to worry only about learning GAAP.

What is Compliance in Accounting?

Compliance means exactly what it sounds like. Rather than trying to break laws or go against the GAAP, you comply with the law and the standards that you are required to. Basically it just means that you will tell the truth, do it in a way that proves you are telling the truth, and thereby remain legal and compliant. This is done so that we never end up on the wrong side of a governmental body such as the SEC.

Famously, the Sarbanes-Oxley Act was put into place in the early 2000s. There were a ton of corporate scandals by that point, many of which arose directly from the way they handled their accounting. In order to reduce the amount of scandals and increase the level of compliance overall, this act was composed of eleven titles. Each of these titles make clear what is required for compliance.

Title 1: The first title brought the Public Company Accounting Oversight Board into existence. This board has the responsibility of keeping watch over the accounting done by firms that offer auditing services to companies that are traded publicly. This board also has the power to discipline companies which are failing to live up to the new processes for compliance with audits that came with the creation of the PCAOB.

Title 2: This title was created in order to reduce conflicts of interest that arose from auditing firms. Firms that were providing auditing were found to also be doing consulting work with the companies that they had been hired to audit. This created a conflict of interest that was completely transparent when brought to light in various scandals. In order to prevent this from happening, this title put standards of compliance in place for external auditors.

Title 3: Now we move into the responsibility of the corporation. The senior executives of a company are now explicitly held accountable for the accuracy of the financial numbers that the corporation reports. If the numbers are wrong and legal action is taken then it is now the CEO's fault. This means that those who are higher up at the company can't pass off responsibility (or blame) to those working beneath them.

Title 4: This title directly increased the principle of full disclosure to set rules in place as to what counted as disclosure and how it was to be provided.

Title 5: No matter how many rules you put in place there is always the chance of a conflict of interest passing through. This title was chosen to prevent conflicts of interest within the world of securities analysts. Now analysts are required by law to disclose any conflicts of interest they might have, that they know of. This title was chosen to help restore the public's confidence in securities analysts. Keep in mind, however, that the phrasing makes it clear that these conflicts are knowable. If a conflict of interest that was unknowable arises then it does not violate this. The best course of action in regards to compliance is to immediately own up to the conflict when it becomes clear.

Title 6: While the previous title required securities analysts to reveal their conflicts of interest, this title sets out how those professionals who work in securities are to act. This title was closely tied to the previous title as both were chosen in order to improve the public's confidence in securities professionals. But another component of this title was making it crystal clear what kind of authority the SEC has over securities analysts. If the SEC needs to, it was made clear that they have the power to discipline analysts. They can even bar them from practicing if they are found to be willfully conflicting with compliance practices.

Title 7: This title required the SEC and the Comptroller General to run a series of studies and make their findings public. Rather than any single topic, the studies they ran covered a range of discussions that ranged from how consolidating public accounting firms would play out to how investment banks factored into the major accounting scandals of the time. Other studies were performed as part of this title, thus completing its purpose. These studies were meant to give those in places of power, as well as investors, a clearer sense of what was happening within the world of corporate accounting.

Title 8: This title is sometimes called the Corporate and Criminal Fraud Act of 2002 and it's a pretty important act to be aware of. One of the problems with compliance was that the laws surrounding it were unclear. What exactly counted as obscuring information to give the illusion of compliance? And with all of these major companies like Enron creating large and well-documented scandals, why didn't anyone come forth sooner?

The problem here is that what could be played off as accidental and what counted as interference in terms of compliance was loosely defined. Furthermore, there wasn't a clear guideline as to what the penalties of these actions would be. What was known at the time, or at least most employees suspected, was that to speak out about what they were seeing would cost their jobs. They were right, too. But this title put in new penalties for interference and created protections for those who are willing to speak out about white collar crime when they encounter it.

Title 9: Speaking of white collar crime, this title also goes by the name of the White Collar Crime Penalty Enhancement Act of 2002. Corporate officers that failed to ensure that their financial reporting was certifiable and replicable now can have criminal charges placed against them. This ties this title closely to the corporate responsibility of title three. Along with increasing who is to be held accountable, this title also increased the penalties for crimes of this type and it especially increased them where conspiracies are concerned. It is a criminal offense to mess up through negligence but it is extremely damaging to be shown to be part of a conspiracy to commit white-collar crime.

Title 10: This title is the easiest of them all to understand. It's also the shortest. Simply put, the CEO of the company must sign every tax return related to the company. What this means is that the CEO of the company is agreeing, through their signature, with the information they are seeing. This means they had to not only have it sent to them so that they could look over it but that they had to physically indicate that they did.

With this title, there is no way for a CEO to say that they weren't aware of what was happening. Either they weren't aware and thus are showing that they are running things extremely poorly and they should not be left in charge, or they are showing that they knew there was a problem and still signed over their information anyway and that points towards conspiracy.

Title 11: The final title is known as the Corporate Fraud Accountability Act of 2002. This made committing fraud on a corporate level a criminal offense. This act also made tampering with financial records into a criminal offense, complete with information on how to sentence these crimes. Furthermore, this act also gave the SEC the ability to freeze transactions which it suspects could be problematic. Financial transactions that seem unusual or larger than normal can be frozen in order to be investigated.

The freezing of transactions comes with pros and cons. For the law-abiding company, a frozen payment is a hassle. It needs to get sorted out and this takes time. This law is troublesome in this case, but when it comes to companies that are trying to succeed at a scam then it can be invaluable. By freezing a transaction, the SEC has a better ability to investigate it as it is still "current." In contrast, a transaction that has already gone through is now in the past and the money has exchanged pockets and will be harder to keep track of.

Compliance: So there you have it. Compliance is simply making sure that we follow the rules, principles and laws surrounding accounting. While it is a simple topic, there is a lot to it. But as you've been reading through, I'm sure you'll notice how the average business that abides by the law isn't going to find it particularly difficult to keep compliant.

Chapter Summary

- There are two key frameworks for accounting: GAAP and IFRS. Both of these are different, with GAAP being much more rules-focused, but they both stress good accounting principles.

- Principles like the revenue recognition principles, the historical cost principle, the matching principle, the full disclosure principle, and the objectivity principle all keep modern-day accountants on the right side of the law and they reduce errors in reading reports.

- The revenue recognition principle is broken surprisingly often considering how easy it is. This principle states that you must record and recognize all your revenue as income. Basically, you can't take a tip without recording it for the books or you're breaking the law. This is an easy mistake to make but it is an extremely dangerous one because it can land you on the wrong side of the law quickly.

- The historical cost principle tells us that we must keep the costs of our assets as they were when purchased. Rather than changing the price of an asset because it has changed since acquisition, you must keep with the historical price. This keeps your records reflecting the money actually spent rather than altering it.

- The matching principle tells us that expenses from revenue must be accounted for in the same period as that revenue even if they weren't paid out yet. If you pay a commission to your employees on sales accounted for in July but don't pay it until August, you would still have to recognise that expense as part of that income even though the money doesn't leave hands yet. It was earned or incurred at the time of the revenue.

- The full disclosure principle states that we will be completely honest with our financial reports, we won't hide any information and we won't try to disguise any information. To put it bluntly, this principle states thou shall not lie on financial statements.

- The objectivity principle reminds us that the information we are sharing is neutral. It is not for us to create a narrative for investors. We aren't telling a story when we are making up our financial statements, we are just reporting the facts as reflected in the balance sheet, the income statement, the cash flow statement, and the statement of retained earnings.

- GAAP stands for Generally Accepted Accounting Principles. These principles are covered in the Federal Accounting Standards Advisory Board's handbook on accounting standards which can be found online at fasb.gov/accounting-standards.

- The GAAP has many, many rules and it is best to use the search function of your PDF reader or browser to search through it for issues related to your business frequently until you get a sense of it.

- Any American accountant should be familiar with the GAAP, which can make hiring a professional accountant an attractive idea.

- IFRS stands for International Financial Reporting Standards. The IFRS is used in most countries while America uses the GAAP.

- The IFRS are much less rule-based than the GAAP and instead they focus on teaching good principles.

- If you are American then you will only need to worry about the GAAP. However, browsing the IFRS can give you an idea of how the rest of the world manages their financial information and this can make you a better investor on the international scale.

- In accounting we must make sure that we comply with the laws and standards as set out by the various governmental bodies.

- The early-2000s saw the Sarbanes-Oxley Act come into effect after some major companies made international headlines for their accounting scandals. This act had eleven titles which together make the rules and regulations around accounting more clear. At the same time the act also increased the penalties for lying and trying to hide money and forging phony financial statements.

In the next chapter you will learn all about financial statements. From the balance sheet to the income statement and from the cash flow statement to the statement of retaining earnings, we'll be looking in depth at the various financial statements that accountants put together in order to maintain compliance and analyze how your company is doing.

CHAPTER FOUR

FINANCIAL STATEMENTS

Financial statements are confusing. Trust me when I tell you that I get it. Learning how to read and use them isn't exactly rocket science but it sure is boring. At least rocket science has, you know, rockets. Financial statements are just numbers and data, not really the type of thing to get excited about.

But they're incredibly important for every business, so we need to set aside our boredom and frustration and figure them out. Once you have you will find that financial statements aren't nearly as intimidating, or even as boring, as they seemed at first.

In this chapter we are going to aim to do just that. We'll start by first going over some key concepts that make it easier to read, understand, and benefit from financial statements. Following that we're going to move into discussions about the various financial statements themselves such as the balance sheet, income statements, cash flow statements, and statement of retaining earnings. This chapter will thus serve as our first deep dive into the statements themselves. As these statements are the main bread-and-butter of accounting, it is important to pay attention and make sure that you grasp the information ahead.

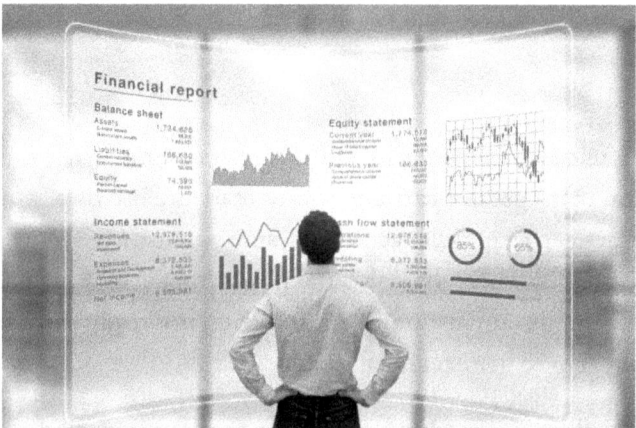

Understanding Financial Statements

Before we look at individual financial statements, it serves us best to look at financial statements as a whole. By approaching them in this manner we can create a framework through which to view them that we can return to whenever we get lost in the numbers and lose sight of our foundation. The key sections of financial statements are the balance sheet, the income statement, and the cash flow statement. Also extremely important are any notes you use to explain what investors are looking at when they consider your statements.

The first thing to understand about financial statements, far before you consider any particular component of them, is their purpose. Financial statements don't particularly make it any easier to run a company. If they are used properly then they can, but if you're dealing with things on a day-to-day basis and keeping tracking of things your own way then nothing is to say the business won't work. Financial statements aren't really for you so much as they are for others. Compliance is important but we're not talking about the government's need for your financial statements. No, instead it is better to consider your investors.

There are limitless investors out there and one or some of them may think that your company is a great idea and they may even consider investing in you. If they do then they are going to want to be able to see that their investment is paying off. Investors want to make sure that they are winning at this game, not losing. To that end, financial statements serve as scorecards that let investors know if they're making points or losing them. What framework an investor uses will determine how they interpret the data but that is an individual thing. In order to have this data they need the scorecard, i.e. your financial statements. Proper financial statements will show exactly where your company's numbers are.

In order to achieve this effect we use the balance sheet, the income statement, and the cash flow statement when performing investment analysis. There might be other tools that people want to see used but these are the key. Of these it is the balance sheet and the income statement that are most often used when making decisions but all three of these statements should be included together. The numbers in these statements represent financial information about how much is being made and how much is being spent, as well as information on the products and services and events that the company deals with or is affected by. These numbers are gathered by sticking to an established framework such as the GAAP so that everyone will be speaking the same language for better transparency.

One thing that we can figure out with a quick look at our financial statements is that they aren't the same. The GAAP helps to keep everything looking similar, in the same mold, but the information that is going to be in one company's financial statements is going to look different from the information in another company's. Business doesn't have a typical appearance. Rather, the world of business has a whole range of possibilities and each one is going to have different needs and they are going to handle them in different ways. This creates a diverse range of information that you could encounter in a financial statement. Don't look for a "standard" balance sheet that you can just copy. You must use your knowledge and experience to put together your own based on the unique circumstances of your company. As a quick addendum to that idea, consider spending some time reading up on financial terms and phrases. It can make it much easier to understand what you are doing or what you are seeing if you speak the lingo.

These statements are thus tools with a specific purpose and a specific way through which they are to be used. If you can wrap your head around them one at a time then you will be able to master the basic accounting skills you need to keep your business running legally, at least until it grows to the point where you need a dedicated accountant.

Balance Sheet

Your company's balance sheet is one of the financial statements which we generate through accounting. They cover a specific period of time and are used to help judge the capital structure of your business or to figure out what your rate of return is. It basically serves as a quick photo of where your company is at a particular point in time in relation to how much the company owes and how much it controls.

We use a simple formula when working on the balance sheet. Assets equal liabilities plus shareholders' equity. This basically means that the company must pay for the things it owns. This money can come from liabilities, such as borrowing money in the form of loans, or from shareholders' equity, i.e. using money provided by investors. If you take a $100 loan then you would have $100 in your assets and $100 in liabilities. If you take $100 from investors then your assets go up by $100 while the shareholders' equity also goes up by $100. When a company earns more money than it has expenses then it is placed in the shareholders' equity category. This is balanced on the assets side in different ways such as cash or company investments or new inventory. The fact that there can be different options for accounting for this new asset is made possible because assets, liabilities, and shareholders' equity all have different sub-categories in which you can note your resources.

Since the balance sheet is simply capturing what is happening with your company's finances at any given moment, it is most valuable when it is compared to balance sheets from earlier periods. Your company also exists within an industry that has competitors you should be following closely. Comparing your balance sheet against theirs can help you to get different ideas on how to run your finances. We talked about assets, liabilities, and shareholders' equity in chapter two but let us touch on them again briefly since these are the three components on the balance sheet.

Your assets are those items that can be turned into cash quickly. Assets include cash or any cash equivalents such as treasury bills. Marketable securities fall under assets, as well as your accounts receivable, your inventory, and any prepaid expenses the company has currently. These are all short-term assets because of how easily they convert to money. Long-term assets include things such as fixed assets like land or machinery, long-term investments, and intangible assets like the favors you are owed or any intellectual property you own.

Liabilities are money that you owe to others. These include short-term accounts such as what debt you have currently, how much you are indebted to the bank, how much interest you owe, your employee's wages or customers prepayments that need to be honored, any dividends you need to pay investors, the premiums that have been earned or that are soon to be, and, finally, your accounts payable. You also have long-term liabilities such as your long-term debt, pension fund liability, and deferred tax liability.

Shareholders' equity is the money that comes from your shareholders. Your retained earnings are added to the shareholders' equity because the shareholders' equity counts as the assets that your company has when liabilities are accounted for. Retained earnings can be used to pay off debts and the remaining money is shared with shareholders as dividends. A company can repurchase shares from shareholders to keep as treasury stock. Shareholders' equity isn't divided into short-term and long-term categories the way assets or liabilities are.

Your balance sheet will start with assets, list all the relevant categories, and come up with a total. It will then list the liabilities and go through the same, followed by the equity. You start at the top of the balance sheet and just read down in a straightforward manner. However, the balance sheet does have its limitations. For one, it only represents a single moment in time. It isn't particularly helpful for getting a sense of how a company has grown over time. As a document on its own there are a lot of ways that someone can read this. The best way to use balance sheets is to compare them and get that sense of what happened over time. There is still room for personal interpretation when this is the case but not to nearly the same degree as alone.

Income Statement

The income statement is sometimes referred to as the profit and loss statement or as the statement of revenue and expense. These alternative names, together with "income statement," really let you know that this statement is all about the money that is coming into and going out from your company. The goal of the income statement is to show your company's financial performance over a specific period of time. The income statement is a bit more complicated than the balance sheet, in my opinion, but it is just as important. We'll look through each of the sections, explore the structure and get a fully rounded grasp on these types of statements before moving onto our cash flow statements.

An income statement begins with a heading that specifies the accounting period it is concerned with. From there it breaks down into four sections: revenue, gains, expenses, and losses. These sections don't see a difference between sales in cash or sales done on credit. It starts with information related to sales and moves down the list until all four sections have been fully explored, at which point it then states the net income for the given period.

The first section is revenues but it is closely tied to the second section, gains, so as to make it most appropriate to look at the two sections together rather than one on one. We'll repeat this with the third and fourth sections for the same reason.

Revenues and gains are required to contain pretty much the same information no matter where you are from but how that information is formatted will be largely due to local restrictions and regulations. There are two types of revenue to be concerned with. The first is operating revenue and it is the revenue that comes from the main activities of your business. If you are in manufacturing then then the main activity would be the selling of goods and this would be where your operating revenue came from. If you are a company offering editing services to authors then your operating revenue would come from your services directly. This is in contrast to non-operating revenue which comes from secondary business activities. This revenue would be things such as rental income or revenue that was generated from interest, things like that. Gains are another form of revenue but one that comes from activities outside of the daily or typical processes of the company. If you were to sell long-term assets then the revenue that they generated would fall under the gains category.

One common problem that people face trying to figure out their income statements is that they confuse revenue with receipts. Revenue isn't directly tied to in-coming cash. Let's say you are putting together an income statement for one quarter. A week before that quarter ends a well-known client comes to you and purchases some goods. Since you know this customer well, you give them a month to make the payment. Their commitment to pay counts as revenue and it would be recorded as such. But it wouldn't be until they paid you the following month that you received the cash itself and thus generated a receipt. Some people get it in their head that they can't have revenue without a receipt but this mistake will result in your accounts being off.

Expenses are those costs that your business incurs while turning a profit. They are broken down into multiple subsections the same way that revenue is. Primary activity expenses are the expenses that you must pay in order to operate the business and earn your primary revenue. These include the costs of the goods you're selling or the cost of administrative expenses or research. Employee wages and sales commissions, even costs like electricity and gas all manage to fall under this category. Ultimately, most of your costs are likely to fall under primary activity. Secondary activity expenses are a much smaller category and they include costs that you pay onto business activities outside of your core. Costs such as interests on loans fall into this section. Losses are another form of expense but one in which the money spent is not going to be recouped. Losses include things like selling long-term assets at a loss or money spent settling lawsuits, basically anything where the money is lost and you won't see it again.

The primary revenue and primary expenses sections make up the core of your business. By looking at these two sections you can get a pretty great sense of how the company is performing in its duties. However, the secondary revenue and secondary expenses categories will give you a sense of how the company is running its other components. You could notice that there is a particularly large amount of secondary income and this could be a sign that the company needs to better manage its funds by investing further into areas like production or marketing or even straight-up expanding to sell a new product or offer a new service. Likewise, too many secondary expenses points towards a company that isn't managing its money so well or that is facing issues figuring out how to keep everything running as smoothly as possible. When reading an income statement, you want to make sure that you read and consider all the parts and not just those in the primary activities sections.

Income statements use these four sections (which in turn are made up of their own subsections) in order to generate a number for the company's net income during the period in question. You must first figure out those sections otherwise it will be impossible to complete the following mathematical formula. Once those section are figured out then the formula you apply to find your net income is:

Net Income = (Revenue + Gains) − (Expenses + Losses)

So let's see this in action using some simple numbers. Let's say you had revenue of $25,000 and gains of $1,000. But in the same period you had expenses of $12,500 and losses of $500. Now we can put this together to get:

Net Income = ($25,000 + $1,000) − ($12,500 + $500)

This in turn gives us:

Net Income = $26,000 - $13,000

And so we can easily solve this to get our net income:

Net Income = $13,000

This is one of those areas in accounting which is easy once you see it broken down but which can be quite complicated when first figuring it out on your own. This is one of those reasons why I always recommend that those who are new to accounting take the time to work through each of their statements at least twice. I want to be clear with this statement: I give you permission to mess up, but you must go through and check your numbers a second time to fix that mess up. If you don't then you will have issues. If you go through twice while still learning then you get more experience filling out your financial statements and you can catch those mistakes before they get sent off.

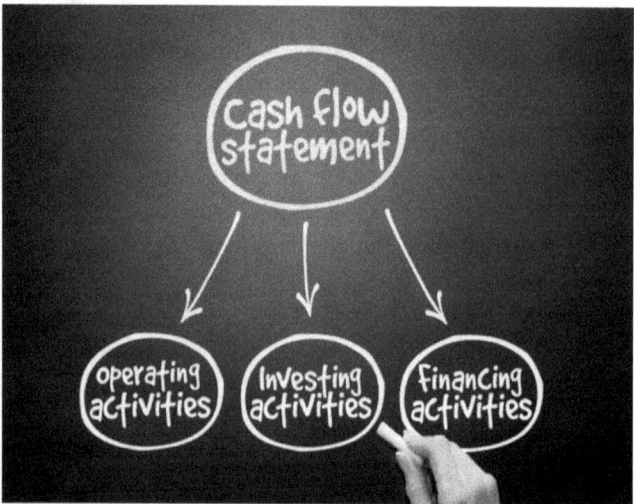

Cash Flow Statement

The cash flow statement's purpose is to summarize how much cash (or cash equivalents) have entered and left the company during the period in question. It, together with the balance sheet and the income statement, completes the financial statements which you are required by law to report. Investors use the cash flow statement to get an understanding of how the company is running, how it is making money, and how it is spending said money. Together with the income statement and the balance sheet, the cash flow statement allows investors to get an unbiased idea of how the company is doing so that they know, without a doubt, that they are happy with investing their money into the company.

A cash flow statement is structured into pieces the same way as any of these financial statements are. As each statement is composed of separate parts, they can be thought of as the sum of their parts and each section can be learned independently before being brought together in the whole. With the cash flow statement, those parts are the cash that comes from operating activities, the cash from investing, the cash from financing, and a disclosure of any noncash activities (which isn't always necessary but those following GAAP need to be sure to look into when it *must* be included). The cash flow statement does not make reference to credit, as the other statements have, but instead focuses exclusively on cash and not on net income. The most confusing of the sections is the cash from operating activities section and so we'll be exploring this first.

Operating activities, in regards to the cash flow statement, are those activities which actually use cash. This shows us how much cash the company has generated through their activities and it would include items like receipts from sales, receipts from services, payments made on interest or income tax, payments made to supplies or wage payments made to employees, payments made on rent, and anything else that could fall under operating expenses (this category can be extremely wide depending on the type of business such as how investment companies include debt and equity instruments). How these come together in calculating cash flow is a bit difficult. There are certain adjustments which are made to net income in order to calculate the cash flow. There are non-cash items that are calculated into a company's net income so these adjustments serve to remove these from the equation so that the cash flow statement focuses entirely on cash. To calculate your cash flow, you need to use either the direct cash flow or the indirect cash flow method.

The direct cash flow method is the easier of the two. It calculates the sum of the cash payments and receipts that the company has. These could include things such as cash that has been paid toward supplies or cash receipts from customers purchasing the company's services and cash that has been paid out to employees as wages. To figure out the sum of all these cash transactions the accountant uses the financial figures from the beginning of the period in question and compares it to the figures from the end of the period. They must look at all of the different business accounts rather than a singular one, of course, but this allows them to see what the net difference is. This net difference could be a positive one or a negative one.

The indirect cash flow method requires the accountant to first check the income statement in order to get the figure for the company's net income. The income statement is calculated and prepared using the accrual basis rather than purely focusing on cash. Remember how we prepared our income statements by noting the money we expected to come in when that customer of ours was given thirty days to pay? This is accrual accounting. We made note of that income when we made the transaction and earned it but not necessarily when it was paid to us. This means that the net income from the income statement is not the same as net cash flow and so we can't just use this number. The accountant needs to make adjustments to the figure from the income statement to figure out the cash flow.

As the accounts receivable on the balance sheet changes in a period, this is shown in the cash flow. If the number decrees on the balance sheet it means that there is more money coming into the company. Since more money has come in then we see the net sales increase by the amount the accounts receivable shrunk. When the number on the balance sheet increases, it means that the net sales see this amount taken away because that revenue is not cash but credit. When the inventory on the balance sheet increases then you need to check to see if it was bought with cash or with credit. If it was bought with cash then that increase on the balance sheet represents cash leaving the company and thus a smaller net sales number is generated. Purchases made on credit result in a higher accounts payable. If this number has changed for the better, the change increases the net sales. This process is added to other payable accounts such as insurance, salaries, or taxes payable. Basically, when something is paid off then we see that as cash leaving the company and a lower net sales but if it hasn't yet then we carry that difference forward as net earnings.

The investing activities part of the cash flow statement is calculated based on activities that change the company's overall assets, investments, or equipment. This section is most often a negative value because it is far more common for a company to purchase assets or equipment then it is for them to profit from selling them. It can happen, of course, but those are typically few and far between. The cash flow from financing activities part of the cash flow statement covers any cash coming or going from banks or investors, plus any cash that has been paid to shareholders in the form of dividends or buybacks. People reading a cash flow statement understand that a positive number represents raising money while a negative number indicates dividends or loans being paid.

Together these various categories will give the cash flow figure for the period in question. Most people automatically think that this number should be a positive, but a negative number isn't necessarily a bad sign. A negative number could be a bad sign but it could also mean that a company is expanding. This would naturally result in more money earned in the long run and thus make the company more attractive. Without further analysis, the negative number will seem quite unattractive. This is one reason why you should look at the financial statements for a company over multiple periods of time rather than just one individual period. It is also a reason why you should consult the balance sheet and the income statements that the company releases too. That way you can always get a full sense of what is happening.

Statement of Retained Earnings

Made in accordance with the GAAP, the statement of retained earnings shows the changes in a company's retained earnings over the period in question. This statement doesn't need to be a full document in the way that the others do, as it can be included on the balance sheet or on the income statement. This document tells the reader how the company's retained earnings has changed, what the net income for the period was, and how much the stockholders were paid in dividends. This will also have information on how the net income will be spent on certain things beyond the dividend payments to investors. We'll go over retained earnings again briefly to see how the statement of retained earnings benefits anyone reading the financial statements released for a given period of time.

Retained earnings come whenever your company makes money. This extra money is often used to make payments on debts or other financial obligations that the company has accumulated. If the company doesn't have any looming debts or is fine with them where they are then this money could be spent to grow the company. The money that a company has in retained earnings will be paid to investors and thus lower the overall amount of retained earnings that a company has. Money beyond what is paid out may be used to expand the company or create and market a new product, maybe it can be used for a merger or to buyback shares or pay off a loan. Pretty much any of the reasons that retained earnings are being spent are positive ones. Though it is best that they are being spent, as too many retained earnings over too long a period of time is a red-flag.

A statement of retained earnings is primarily designed to instill confidence in investors. It shows the investor how the retained earnings are being used to continue promoting company growth. The investor will be able to tell how much of their earnings the company is retaining. This is often called the retention ratio. This is simply how much much money the company is retaining for growth compared to how much they are paying out to investors. Investors see a company that is spending all of its earnings on outbound payments as risky. This tells them that the company might struggle to grow any larger. A company that keeps money for growth could be a sign of a good investment that will improve after purchase. Remember, however, that holding onto money for too long without reinvesting in the company is also a bad look. It's a bit hard to figure out how to walk the right way for investors but so long as you are committed to your company this shouldn't be a problem in the long run. Company growth is always attractive.

Chapter Summary

- Financial statements are one of the most important components of accounting simply due to the fact that you are legally required to provide them.

- Financial statements are generated and distributed in order to give investors a sense of where the company is. They allow an investor to see if they like the way the company is doing and they can decide if they want to stay on board with the company, buy more shares, or sell theirs based on the information in the financial statements.

- While financial statements are important, they aren't perfect documents. One investor can read one as positive while another reads it as negative. It depends on what standard the investor is looking to judge the company by.

- The numbers used in your financial statements must follow the GAAP. A benefit of this is that investors don't need to learn a unique system of accounting to see where you stand but rather they can easily and directly compare your company to any other.

- We use four financial statements to achieve this objective: the balance sheet, the income statement, the cash flow statement, and the statement of retained earnings.

- The balance sheet covers a specific period of time and shows a quick photo of where the company is at any one given time.

- The balance sheet is made up with the accounting equation of assets equal liabilities plus shareholders' equity.

- The balance sheet is best used when it can be compared to previous balance sheets that the company has generated. This allows investors to see how the company is functioning long-term rather than just a single image in time.

- Assets are items that can be turned into cash. Liabilities are money that you owe others and shareholders' equity is the money that comes from the shareholders and where your retained earnings reside.

- The balance sheet starts with assets and lists them all out in their different subcategories. Then it moves into liabilities and does the same before doing the same yet again with the equity. You can read a balance sheet from the top to the bottom to get a sense of how these different categories have shifted.

- The income statement is sometimes called the profit and loss statement. This statement shows a company's financial performance over a period of time.

- The income statement is broken down into revenue, gains, expenses, and losses.

- Revenue is the money that comes into your company through your main activities. Gains is money that comes into the company from activities beyond the scope of your typical business day such as when you sell long-term assets.

- Revenue is not the same as receipts. Receipts are directly tied to incoming cash. If you are owed $100 that you are expecting to get paid on Wednesday then that would still count as revenue because you already did the work and are owed that. It would not have a receipt yet and it wouldn't count as cash but it is revenue.

- Expenses are costs that a business incurs when making money. Having to pay employees or pay gas for transportation or purchase raw materials are all expenses. Losses are for expenses that incur outside of regular business activities such as when you sell long-term assets at a loss.

- Net income is figured out with the equation: **Net Income = (Revenue + Gains) − (Expenses + Losses)**.

- The cash flow statement tells the reader how much cash or cash equivalents the company has. This does not count money that is coming in at a later date the way that revenue does but rather it focuses on money that is in the form of cash only.

- Operating activities on a cash flow statement show activities which use cash and it shows how much has come in from things like sales or how much has left in the form of payments.

- The direct cash flow method calculates the sum of cash payments and receipts that the company has and uses the financial figures from earlier in the period to see what's changed.

- The indirect cash flow method requires the accountant to check the income statement to get the net income and then go through the documentation and numbers to remove anything that isn't cash and come up with an amount.

- The statement of retained earnings is made to the standards of the GAAP and it can be attached to a balance sheet or income statement.

This document tells the reader how much money you are holding onto.

- A company that doesn't hold onto any extra money is likely not going to grow much more and investing in them represents a riskier investment. A company that holds onto too much money also isn't showing confidence or skill in their ability to grow as a company.

- A good company saves up money to pay back equity or grow the company and so you can expect to see them holding onto money enough to get to a point where they can invest in their own growth.

In the next chapter you will learn about the point at which bookkeeping and accounting meet in the modern day. Recording transactions used to be the realm of bookkeeping but more and more accounting software has been taking over this responsibility and leaving it in the lap of accountants. We'll look at the general ledger, how trial balance is used, how we calculate for and record debits and credits, and how journal entries help us to achieve our accounting goals.

CHAPTER FIVE

RECORDING TRANSACTIONS

When people refer to bookkeeping a lot of the time what they mean is making sure the general ledger is up to date. This is the book where the financial records for the company are stored and it is directly involved in good accounting practices. Since bookkeeping and accounting are becoming more and more tightly woven together it is important for the accountant to understand how to record transactions and keep accurate records.

In this chapter we'll focus on doing just that. We'll start by looking at the general ledger and then move into a discussion on the role of trial balances. From there we'll discuss how we make use of debits and credits before we finish with a discussion on recording journal entries. Together these four sections will give you a quick but thorough understanding of how financial records and transactions are structured and stored for later use.

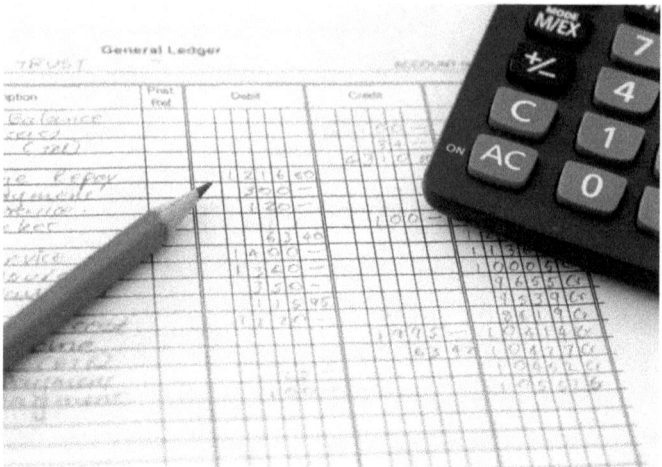

What is a General Ledger?

Back in the day, long before computers, transactions had to be written down in ink and kept up by hand. To keep all of these transactions in the same place, the general ledger was invented. This book let business owners keep track of their finances with ease. In order to keep them accurate and account for possible human error, the general ledger is kept using the double-entry method. This became less important as computers took care of things and made it easier but the general ledger has remained.

Most businesses use the double-entry accounting system, though they don't have to. You can personally use the single-entry accounting system if you really want to but it isn't recommended. The double-entry system is much better because it helps to increase the accuracy, but the general ledger for your company absolutely uses the double-entry system. This simply means that accounts are connected to each other so that an entry into the system in one account represents an opposite entry in a different account. Debits and credits balance each other out in this manner. We'll be looking at credits and debits shortly. We'll also be looking at journals, which are directly tied to the general ledger though they represent the step before data is recorded in the ledger.

Some companies don't use a general ledger but I want to recommend that you do, so let's get into those recommendations.

Why Use a General Ledger?

The most obvious reason for a general ledger is the fact that it lets you keep track of all your financial transactions. Using the general ledger will allow you to ensure that your financial transactions are recorded correctly and the double-entry system gives you extra comfort in knowing they're accurate.

A general ledger is useful in helping a business compile a trial balance, something that we'll be looking at in more detail in just a moment. Beyond that it also makes it easier to get your taxes done up since all of the information is kept in the same location. The less you need to go scrambling for a receipt at the last second, the easier your taxes will be. A general ledger is also good for getting a sense of how your company is managing its budget and you'll be able to get numbers on how much money you're spending and where so that you can adjust the budget with concrete numbers.

Another great thing about a general ledger is that it makes it easier to spot weird transactions and spot fraud. A lot of the time issues with fraud get by because there is not a system in place to spot it. Some cases can go years before getting caught simply because there weren't accurate records being kept of the company's financial records. Keeping a general ledger from the start is a good idea because it instills good healthy and honest record keeping and it makes it harder for fraud to happen and it gets a thousand times easier to spot when it does. Even if you can't prevent it, the sooner you spot it the sooner you can deal with it.

A general ledger isn't necessarily something that you might need for your company but it is one of those things that you can truly benefit from using anyway. As the company grows you'll find that it comes to be even more handy and it is always easier to learn how to use a general ledger in the beginning when things are slower than when things are zooming around you and you're trying to manage your employees, expand your business, and learn how to use a general ledger all at the same time.

What Is a Trial Balance and How Does It Play a Role in Accounting?

The trial balance has one of those names that can make you nervous. Don't worry, nobody is putting you on trial and this has nothing to do with breaking the law. Instead this is a trial in the sense that it is a short, quick, and easy way to see if your accounts are looking good without having to crunch all of the numbers at once.

A trial balance is done by taking the balances of all the accounts in your company's general ledger. Some accounts will have a balance of zero and these can be left out or included, they really won't make a difference in this particular exercise. Accounts are broken up into debit accounts and credit accounts and the amount from each account is placed into the appropriate section. After all the accounts have been divided into these two sections they are totalled. If things are going properly then the amount in the debit balances and the amount in the credit balances sections will be the same.

A trial balance is in no way a financial statement. Instead it is used for internal accounting and bookkeeping purposes to see if there is a problem somewhere. When the accounts don't line up in a trial balance then there could be an issue in what was reported, there could be a mistake in the account balances somewhere, or a credit might have been mislabelled as a debit, or the opposite may have happened. Most accounting software will spot these issues for you ahead of time and this makes the trial balance exercise less useful, but if you are working by hand then checking the trial balance will be more important and you should make running a trial balance a weekly or even a daily goal depending on how much business your company sees.

Understanding Debits and Credits

Debits and credits are one of the more confusing areas of accounting but they are the cornerstone of the double-entry system. I believe that the reason people have such trouble with debits and credits is not because of how they function but rather the names they have been given. Debit brings to mind debit cards and credit brings to mind credit cards and customer credit, but they mean different things when it comes to keeping track of financial transactions.

The easiest way to break down debits and credits is:

Debits represent money flowing in.

Credits represent money flowing out.

Debits are on the left. Credits are on the right.

To understand this in action, let's look at an example. Your company is broken up into all sorts of different accounts. You earn money working for the day and you put the cash you earned into the cash account. This would be a debit of the amount equal to how much you put into the cash account. If you take $1000 out of the cash account to purchase a new computer then this would be a credit of $1000 to the cash account because the money is coming out. But since the money is buying a computer, the computer is an asset and that $1000 would be debited into the account relating to equipment. This means that the cost in cash was removed from the company but converted into the equivalent amount as an asset.

Keep in mind that not every account is a positive one. The accounts used to purchase the computer are accounts that track the assets the company has. There are accounts that are used for tracking the company's liabilities such as when you have an account for loans you've taken from the bank. When you are dealing with an account like this then you would debit your cash account for the amount you gained in the loan but you would also credit your loan account because it is a liability. It represents an amount you have to pay rather than the amount you have of something. We see this happen the same way when dealing with equity raised by investors. The cash section gets debited but the equity account is credited. Equity accounts go up when they are credited because they measure what investors have in your company rather than anything your company has itself.

Debits and credits can remain pretty difficult so try to keep these tips in mind.

1.   Debits raise asset accounts but credits lower them.

2.   Debits raise expense accounts but credits lower them.

3.   Debits lower liability accounts but credits raise them.

4.   Debits lower equity accounts but credits raise them.

5.   Debits lower revenue but credit increases it.

6.   Debits are always recorded on the left with credits recorded on the right.

Recording Journal Entries

Journal entries in accounting is more of a method of recording an accounting transaction than it is a way of leaving detailed notes like you might think of when you think of a personal journal. Regardless, a good accountant can read journal entries of this type with just as much clarity. Journal entries are often worked into the general ledger but they are sometimes divided into smaller ledgers that will then be added to the general ledger at a later date. These journal entries make the world of accounting much easier.

The journal entries used in accounting must be at least two lines long. They can be longer than this, as there is no limit to how many can be included so long as there are at least two at the beginning. A journal entry that has only two entries is a simple journal entry while those with more than two items are called compound journal entries. While it might seem natural to think that putting as much information onto an entry at a time would be the best approach this isn't always the case. Often it is actually easier to take about a particular piece of information when it stands on its own and can easily be referenced when it is needed.

So… what is a journal entry?

Simply put, a journal entry is the way that we record debits and credits. Those annoying things from just a minute ago? Yup, them. The reason that there has to be at least two lines to an entry is because you must balance out a debit with a credit. The amount of money in any journal entry, or transaction, must equal out when the debits and credits are compared to each other. If they don't equal out then your accounts aren't balanced and there is a problem somewhere.

A journal entry must show both of the accounts involved, the one getting the debit and the one getting the credit. The date must be recorded. You must also take note under which accounting period the entry is being made. A journal entry must have the name of the person making the entry. If the person making the entry is not a manager then it must have a manager's signature. The journal entry must be given a number for further reference. It must be noted whether or not the entry is a one time thing or if it is a repeating entry and any documentation related to the entry should be included. At the very least a journal entry should have a short paragraph, even just a couple of sentences, about what the journal entry represents.

While this is what your journal entries must have at a minimum, there are different types of journal entries. The common journal entry is a one time entry and it can be noted fairly easily. A reversing journal entry is one that is reversed, as the name implies. A recurring journal entry is one that will recur in multiple accounting periods and it typically needs to be given a termination date in order to finish.

These tools are easy to use, simply record the debits on the left and the credits on the right and always make sure there are at least two sections. It is easiest to write down the list of requirements for a journal entry and keep them on a sticky note for quick reference. They're not so much complicated as they are tedious to remember so keeping them near at hand will make recording your journal entries that much easier.

Chapter Summary

- Recording transactions is technically the realm of bookkeeping but it is important for accountants to learn as these two roles become more closely related.

- A general ledger is a book which keeps track of all the financial transactions for a company. The general ledger may have all of the accounts listed in it or it may have sections of the company's accounts broken down into smaller ledgers which themselves are stored within the general ledger.

- The general ledger keeps all of the financial information in one location so that it is easy to reference it as it is needed for accounting purposes.

- A general ledger requires the double-entry accounting system in order to function. This means that when an entry is made in an account, there is another equal entry in a related account. By using the double-entry accounting system it is easier to keep everything balanced and in order.

- The general ledger allows you to compile a trial balance.

- One of the best aspects of a general ledger is the way that it lets you catch weird transactions early and spot fraud. By being aware of financial transactions as they happen it is easier to catch the weird ones while there are still options for how to deal with them.

- You might think that there is no value to using a general ledger in your company if it is quite small but the sooner you do, the better it is. Getting used to working with a general ledger can get you and your managers thinking about finances earlier and this is always a positive for a business.

- A trial balance is a way of quickly seeing if your accounts are balanced without having to do any heavy lifting. A trial balance takes all of the company's accounts and divides them into debit accounts or credit accounts. Each category gets totalled together and it is expected that credit and debit accounts will equal each other out. If they don't then there is a problem that must be fixed.

- A trial balance is not a financial statement. Instead it should be considered as a quick tool for checking if the accounts are balanced. Beyond this it doesn't offer much value in the long-run. Rather, it is a way to save yourself some work. If everything is balanced then the accountant can rest easy. If it isn't then there is work to be done and a problem to solve.

- Debits and credits are confusing in accounting because they don't have anything to do with debit or credit as it is typically thought of.

- Debits in accounting represent money flowing into an account.

- To credit an account represents money that is flowing out.

- Debits and credits are listed in the general ledger. Debits are always on the left and credits are always on the right.

- Debits raise asset accounts and expense accounts. Credits lower asset accounts and expense accounts.

- Debits lower liability accounts and equity accounts. Credits raise liability accounts and equity accounts.

- Debits lower revenue, credit raises revenue.

- Not every account is a positive one. Some accounts are increased by crediting such as accounts that represent equity. Taking out more money debits the account it moves the money into and it credits the account representing loans (or however the money was generated). Because the higher a number in an equity account, the more that is owed, a credit to this account represents an increase in the amount owed. A credit represents money leaving an account but so does this account. The higher the number in the account, the more money you owe and thus the more money that is ultimately leaving in tune to the transaction.

- Journal entries are a way of recording an accounting transaction in the general ledger. A journal entry must be at least two lines long. The first line records the debit, the second line records the credit. Two lines is the minimum it takes to properly record a journal entry for a double-entry system.

- A journal entry can be as long as you want it to be but it is better to record multiple short entries than to record one long entry. Since each entry is given a unique number for later reference, it is easier to find the information you need when it is labelled on its own rather than as part of something larger.

- Each journal entry must show the accounts involved, the date it is recorded, the accounting period it is for, the name of the person making the entry, the manager's signature, a unique number for later reference, a note on whether the entry is one time or recurring, and any additional documentation that is necessary for record keeping purposes.

- A one-time entry is the most common. A recurring journal entry is one that repeats in later accounting periods and typically it must be stopped manually or it will continue to recur. A reversing journal entry is one that is reversed and thus is used for fixing errors and the like.

In the next chapter you will learn about managerial accounting. You've already seen that this type of accounting is used to generate reports that are used internally rather than externally but it's now time to put these ideas into action in order to create budgets, run margin analyses and cash flow analyses, forecast your findings, and calculate your financial leverage.

CHAPTER SIX

MANAGERIAL ACCOUNTING

For our last chapter in this introduction to accounting we are going to look at managerial accounting. This form of accounting, as discussed in chapter one, is entirely focused on generating reports and data that help with the internal running of the company. The reports that we make in managerial accounting are not intended to be read by anyone outside of the company and there is no one right or wrong way to generate them. If you make a mistake in your managerial accounting then you are going to have a rough time trying to run the company off faulty data but you aren't going to end up on the wrong side of the law.

With that said, we must make note of the importance of keeping our managerial accounting in line with itself. If we decide to make use of managerial accounting then we must create guidelines to follow that keeps all of our financial data looking the same. Financial accounting has the GAAP and IFRS to keep it in line but these can be thrown out the window for managerial accounting. But just because they can doesn't mean that they should. It is better to stick with the principles that your company uses in their financial accounting. Doing so will ensure that your internal reports can be read and compared to your external reports. This isn't important for investors or anything but it can help to provide your managers and yourself with as much data as possible.

I am of the mindset that when it comes to running your business, data is the most important thing in the world. The more data you can have, the better you can understand the situation you find yourself in at any given moment. I also believe that to keep up with all of your financial data on a regular basis is a great way to spot fraud or errors early and prevent them from causing long-term damage, which happens when a small error goes unnoticed and is allowed to snowball and grow larger each new reporting period.

This chapter focuses on those managerial accounting tools that all beginners need to learn. They include the basics like budgeting and forecasting, margin analysis and cash flow analysis, and a look at financial leverage. Once you have a solid grasp of these skills you will be ready to start applying them to your company to see how they work in action to give you more knowledge and a better understanding of your company's accounting.

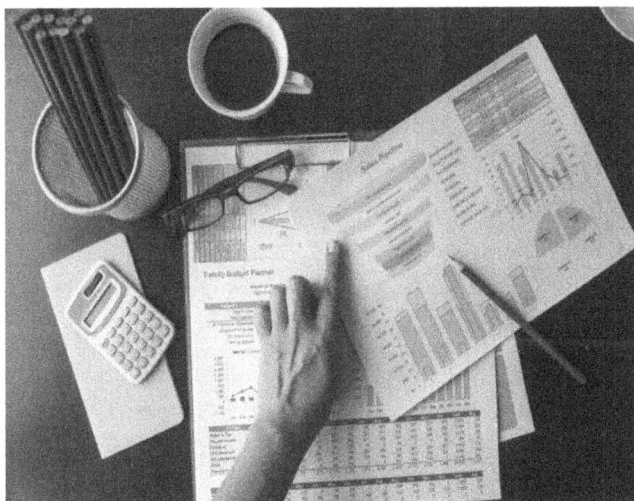

Budgeting

Budgets are one of the most important tools that your company's managers can have. Most people think they understand what a budget is but there are actually a few different types that we'll be looking at. Before we get into types, let's just set down a basic definition to begin with. A budget, in managerial accounting, is any document which sets out goals for the use of finances during a given period of time. That period of time could be a day, a week, a month, a quarter, a year, or more. The when of it is less important than the concept that a budget is a guideline for how to spend money.

There are many reasons that your company should use a budget. In fact, there are many reasons why each and every person reading this should have a budget, even just a personal one. We'll stick to the benefits that they provide to your company in this book. One of the biggest things a budget does for a company is give the management of the company the ability to look ahead and make goals and plans. A budget gives you a sense of where the money is going at any given time, or rather it gives you a sense of where the money is supposed to go. Just because we make a budget doesn't mean that we are going to follow it. We are supposed to but it is very easy to make mistakes and spend where we aren't supposed to. If we make a budget then the idea inherent in that is that we are going to stick to it. If we do stick to it like we are supposed to then we absolutely can use a budget to give a sense of where our finances are going to be in the future and we can make plans for how to use them. A budget makes growing your company easier.

A budget also helps managers to get the company's spending under control and to be more involved in each part of the company. For example, you might have managers that spend all of their time out on the floor looking over the employees and convincing customers to purchase goods. Meanwhile the shipping department is being run pretty much manager-free. The manager might have no idea how much money is actually being used by the department. Once you have a budget in place, the department knows exactly how much money they have to spend and if they need more then they will have to come talk to someone about it. Rather than money simply leaving the company, the budget helps to put limits on the amount and foster discussion between the various departments of the company. As discussions between the various departments take off it helps to create a sense of togetherness through the company rather than creating bubbles of isolation.

Budgets are also useful in getting your managers more into the mindset of the accountant. While you don't necessarily want your managers to be accountants themselves, you do want them to be aware of the reality of financial transactions, keeping good records, and considering the company's finances before making decisions. These are all good practices for your managers to be accustomed with. The more your managers understand the financial side of the company, the better they get at working with the company that way. Even more important is that a financially educated manager is a manager who is much more likely to spot some kind of fraud or issue. The perfect company would never deal with fraud or financial problems but this is simply an unrealistic standard to try to live by. Instead it is best to teach your managers so that their eyes become watchful for the signs of problems in their early stages.

There are several types of budgets and it can be valuable to see the differences between them. Many people think of a budget as being a singular thing but it all depends on how it is built.

A master budget falls in line with what people typically think of when they hear the word. This is a budget that projects how each and every aspect of the business is going to run over the period of the budget. Most of the time a master budget is made for a period of a year but this isn't always the case. A new company might find it more valuable to create a master budget on a quarterly basis, as the company could easily fold before the end of a year if it isn't careful. A master budget creates a cash budget, an income statement, and a balance sheet that has been budgeted. A lot of the time a master budget can be composed of smaller budgets from each of the different departments within the company. By connecting smaller budgets into the master budget it helps to keep each department on the same page. That said, this is definitely an approach favored more by larger companies than smaller ones.

A cash flow budget is one that looks at how cash flows into and out of the business daily. This budget is used to predict how much money the company will make with the goal of showing that the company makes more than it loses. Managers can use this to get a sense of how the income is doing compared to costs like production. It also gives managers a sense of when the inventory needs to be restocked.

An operational budget that covers revenue and expenses is a daily budget that focuses on the company's primary business. Operating budgets like this are made for a year or a larger period of time and then broken down into shorter periods. Managers are able to use the operation budget that covers revenue and expenses similarly to the cash flow budget, but it has a wider net for the data it concerns itself with.

These are just a few of the types of budgets that a company may want to make up. There are lots of other types of budgets but they push beyond the realm of the beginner accountant and start to get into much more complex territory. It is important to remember for the time being that your company will benefit from a budget. You might want to simple set limitations around spending or you may want to get more involved and run multiple types of budgets. You don't need to jump off into the deep end right away but you should begin using budgets as early as possible for the best results and the highest level of control over your company's finances.

Marginal Analysis

Marginal analysis is a bit of a tricky one. It is the name we give to the examination of the benefits of an activity compared to the additional costs of that activity. These benefits can be wide-ranging, as many activities aren't particularly useful for generating cash. For example, marketing your product with an Instagram influencer doesn't directly bring you back money but the promotion is a benefit for your company that must be considered. Marginal analysis is most often used in determining hiring decisions or product production decisions such as "Does hiring another worker make us back more money than we spend paying them?" or "Does it make more sense to order 10 copies of this product or 20? 50? 100?" These are cases where marginal analysis is used to figure out the answer.

The idea behind marginal analysis is that small changes have big effects. We've discussed this idea again and again from a negative perspective such as when we make mistakes in our bookkeeping and it comes back to haunt us. Marginal analysis is a way of testing out these small changes in a neutral setting. The idea here is that each part of the company is just part of a larger system. This system often consists of systems within systems such as when you have multiple departments in the company. When you want to make a change in any one part of the system there is going to be a ripple effect that changes the rest of the system. This ripple can be for the best or for the worse but regardless of which it still happens. Rather than simply introduce the change into the system as it is, marginal analysis gives us a way of testing out this change to see what happens before we commit to it.

Marginal analysis weighs the costs and the benefits of the change to see what happens. Sometimes a change seems necessary, such as hiring a new employee, but a marginal analysis reveals that the cost would be too high compared to the benefits. One place where marginal analysis really shines is where you are faced with more than one option you have to choose from. Let's say you can invest in one improvement to the company but that's all. Marginal analysis will help you to figure out which choice is going to be the most beneficial to the company as a whole. It is achieved easily enough; just take your current financial information and change the numbers to reflect the next situation you are considering. Increase the amount of money being spent and likewise increase the amount of inventory, employees, or whatever it is that you are increasing. This gives you new data that you can use in forecasting to see if the choice is the one that benefits the company the most. Remember to run marginal analysis for each of the options you are considering, not just one. It is only through multiple analyses that you can find the best solution.

Marginal analysis is only focused on a single change at a time. Because of this it can be easy to try out one change and see that it would have a positive impact. Seeing a positive impact, it would be easy to consider the day done early and just go with that one positive. But marginal analysis does not help you choose which options are better. It only allows you to highlight one change. While the first change you explore may be positive that doesn't mean that it is the best change. So, again, consider marginal analysis as a process in which you must go through all the choices you are weighing in order to find which one is the best.

Also remember that marginal analysis is not the end-all-be-all of managerial accounting techniques. It can be an extremely useful tool but it is not some powerful game changer. It comes from the economic theory of marginalism and this theory has been criticized in the past for being rather hard to contain. One of the things that marginalism requires is for the markets to be perfect and this just isn't how the world works. Markets are anything but perfect, especially these days. However, while marginalism isn't a perfect theory it does give us marginal analysis and this tool is powerful. You shouldn't purely rely on marginal analysis for making your decisions; after all, marginal analysis could reveal that the best choice is to let go of somebody or hire somebody new when you know that it isn't the right time. Marginal analysis should be considered a tool but it is still up to the administrative staff in the company to make the calls. Sometimes a gut feeling proves to be more valuable than all the hard data in the world or anything that comes up in a marginal analysis.

Being flexible is important. Make use of marginal analysis in your company but don't treat it like some oracle with all the answers. You're still the one who ultimately has to weigh the pros and cons of all the decisions made on behalf of the company.

Cash Flow Analysis

Cash flow analysis is the analysis of the cash flow statement. This statement is one of the four key financial statements that we looked at in chapter four. In that chapter we looked at how the cash flow statement helps investors to see what is happening with the excess cash your company has generated. While you must learn to use the cash flow statement for external purposes, this is one of those documents which can be just as useful when used internally. One of the biggest issues that smaller companies face is running out of cash. When there's no money left it's awfully difficult to run a company. Performing regular cash flow analysis is a good way to ensure that you are never caught unawares by a cash problem.

The cash flow statement is a financial statement which shows how money comes into and leaves your business during the period in question it represents. This document is extremely important, legally, but it is just as important for you. You may have to provide a cash flow statement for a given period of time but that doesn't mean it is the only one you have to generate. Generating cash flow statements at more regular intervals is always a smart idea.

A cash flow statement is already a smart choice to generate because it provides a snapshot of the way cash is flowing into or out of the company. This doesn't particularly help you out much if you can't analyze it. Cash flow analysis allows you to tell if your cash is looking good or not, if you will have problems making payments or not. By performing cash flow analysis you will be able to tell if you need to adjust your budget or make changes to your cash flow. If the analysis shows a shortage then you can plan for it, if it shows excess cash then you start to contemplate where it should be spent such as in the budget for new equipment or the like. Cash flow analysis performed on a regular basis is the secret weapon your business has so that it never finds itself unable to pay a bill or keep up with an expense.

Before you can analyze your cash flow you first need a cash flow statement. For more information on a cash flow statement, see chapter four. With the cash flow statement made you can then analyze it. This is easier than generating the cash flow statement in the first place. Start by looking at the cash flow from operations section of the cash flow statement. Your goal with the cash flow from operations section is to see the number increase as often as possible. If the number is staying the same or getting smaller then there is an issue with cash flow in your basic operations. Next you should identify how much of your revenue is still yet to be paid by customers. This gives you a sense of what cash you can expect to see coming shortly. Keep an eye on any cash that is being spent on new equipment or the like as this cash should be earned back in future statements because of the increased efficiency of the company due to the new acquisition.

As you move through your cash flow analysis, these are just a few of the areas that you will want to keep your eye on. What we are looking for with an analysis is to really see where the money is going and to spot patterns whenever possible. Humans are creatures of habit and patterns and this means we're actually really great at spotting them. If we're doing regular cash flow analyses then we will be able to see these patterns and learn from them. You could think that money is good until right around the time that the bills are due and this has caused issues. You could use this knowledge to change the way you are handling your money so that you aren't short when it comes to bills and you don't need to make late payments anymore. You could also see patterns that help to inform your decisions around staff payroll or overspending on inventory or when to make bill payments or how effective your marketing has been. You could learn more about when to raise your prices and when to stop extending credit to certain customers. There is a lot that you can learn from cash flow analysis.

So next time you generate a cash flow statement, take the time to break it down and really analyze it. Make this step a part of your regularly scheduled managerial accounting and you will find it proves to be beyond beneficial.

Forecasting

Forecasting is the process through which accountants use data about both current and historical costs in order to predict what something will cost in the future. Forecasting is important because it helps us to better plan our company's future by taking an educated guess as to how much it will cost to continue running primary operations. Forecasting allows us to better create our budgets and thus it has the added benefit of helping us to more fully and accurately make use of our other managerial accounting tools. Since we already looked at budgeting in this chapter we won't have a second discussion on it. Just know that budgeting is one of the tools that combines with forecasting in order to truly level up.

Another tool that forecasting gives us access to is called the high-low method. This method is used for estimating costs through forecasting. It is quite simple and this makes it easy to learn but that simplicity does come at a cost. Because the high-low method is simple, it necessarily isn't the most accurate approach we can use. The easier something is in accounting, the less information it is using. This is a rule of thumb and there are clear examples that break it but for the most part you can trust it. The key to understanding this result is simply to consider how complicated business truly is. As soon as you start to remove data, you start to lose accuracy. That doesn't make it useless. If you are looking to forecast quickly then the high-low method is the go-to approach.

Basically the high-low method uses extremes of data to forecast. You must have data about the costs and the cost-driver activities that are relevant to your company. The high-low method requires us to take the highest cost and the highest cost-driver activity level, as well as the lowest cost and lowest level of cost-driver activity. Once we have these pieces of data we can then use them to calculate what they would like graphed out and connected with a single line. We're interested in discovering what the slope of the line between them is. This slope and one of the four data points are used together to figure out where the intercept is located. Once it is found you have the information for the high-low cost equation of the activity that you are forecasting.

Another approach is called regression analysis. This form of analysis figures out how much variance in a dependent variable is due to the variations in an independent variable. This is a harder form of analysis that is best handled with technology rather than by hand. Regression analysis can be done for a single set of independent and dependent variables or it can be done across multiple. Regardless of how many variables there are in play, regression analysis requires data about both variables to be provided. The end result of regression analysis is an equation that is used in forecasting. This equation is used to help forecast costs based on the information revealed about the independent variable.

Basically, forecasting is a way of estimating data more accurately. You could assume that you understand how much it costs to run your business over a given period but those costs are prone to change as the world changes, as manufacturing changes. There is a whole world of change which comes together to affect the cost of maintaining your business. While forecasting does not allow us to overcome these changes, it is helpful. We can't forecast major world-changing events like a global pandemic or a recession but we can look at how prices have changed throughout our history with them and use this to predict how they will continue to change in the future.

Forecasting is not future-sight. There is no look into the future to see how it will play out. Rather, it is a way of future prediction; it predicts that things will continue to change in accordance to how they've already changed. By accounting for change in this manner we can get a better understanding of what is in store for our company and this allows us to more accurately budget for and react to changes as we face them. It doesn't prepare us for the extraordinary but it does prepare us for the predictable aspects of the future.

Financial Leverage

Financial leverage is the name we give to the practice of using debt to purchase assets. We use financial leverage to increase how much we make from equity. For example, an investor gives $100 to the company. In order to leverage that money you use the $100 to purchase a new printer that allows you to print out merchandise at twice the speed you could previously. Now that $100 will be able to make you back much more than $100 and it means you have a larger return on equity thanks to it. The problem with this approach is that to stretch yourself out too far with too much financial leverage is not a good thing and it can often be a sign that a company is going to fail in the future. Too much leverage makes it harder to repay the core debt and this can signal failure.

Financial leverage is determined by a ratio that compares total debt to total assets. The amount of debt to assets increases in tune with the amount of financial leverage your company is said to have. It is no surprise that the best use of financial leverage is when you are sure that the use will generate back more revenue than the debt you've incurred to spend on it. Financial leverage has an advantage over raising more equity capital because it doesn't lower the earnings per share of the shares that stockholders' already own. Financial leverage can make it so that your company earns more on assets or it can increase the amount of interest you have on your equity and this is sometimes of benefit for reducing your company's taxable income so that you can land in a cheaper tax bracket.

Although financial leverage can help you to earn back a disproportionate amount, it can also cause you to lose this as well. It is important that you consider fully how much interest you will have to expend thanks to financial leverage. You shouldn't use financial leverage on any projects or purchases that aren't going to increase your earnings enough to cover the higher interest rate. It is also important to consider how financial leverage can affect the investors looking at your company. Financial leverage often results in large changes in a company's profits and this can make the price of company shares less organized. Stocks that are more volatile are often more valuable and so this can be a good thing but it can cause issues such as when shares are issued to company employees.

Financial leverage can be a risky way to approach your business. Figuring out when you want to make use of financial leverage and when it is best avoided can be hard to do. There tends to be a limit of financial leverage. There isn't any set rule or anything like that but rather financial leverage requires equity and those that lend money are naturally less likely to lend money to someone that already owes a lot.

Financial leverage is a way that allows a company to use the debt it has acquired to earn more money but it is a risky maneuver because by design it requires the company to increase its debt. If you don't increase your debt, you can't leverage it financially. The safest bet is always to ensure that the money you are using to purchase assets is money that the company is making rather than money it has to borrow.

Business isn't always about taking the safest route. Sometimes you need to take risks, that's just the way it is. But you shouldn't take risks without first being prepared. Before you start making plans for leveraging your finances, take a moment to create a budget, run some margin analysis. Take the time to estimate whether or not the path in front of you is the most beneficial for your company. At the very least you must figure out how badly you will be impacted by the higher interest if your plan to earn enhanced revenue fails. If you can't survive your plan failing then you shouldn't bother with financial leverage. It is too risky.

If you can survive your plan failing, then give it a try. Your goal is never to have the plan fail, so hopefully it won't even matter. You want to ensure that it can before you go ahead, however. As long as it can, you don't need to worry about the company failing beneath you because of poor financial leveraging decisions.

Chapter Summary

- Managerial accounting is the type of accounting that focuses on generating financial information for use within the company. Managers make use of the reports generated through managerial accounting to make accurate and informed decisions about the company's finances.

- Managerial accounting does not need to stick to the GAAP or IFRS the same way that financial accounting does. Since the reports that managerial accounting generate are for internal use, there is no template that must be followed for legal purposes.

- Budgeting is a practice that is beneficial on the personal level but your company absolutely should be making use of budgets. Budgets are simple guidelines for how the company should be and plans to spend its money. A budget helps to reduce overspending.

- A company benefits from a budget for the reduction in overspending but also by the way it gives the reader a clear view of how the company is spending its money. A budget is also useful for connecting various departments together. A manager might not have much reason to speak to a particular department but if there is a budget in place then that department must get authorization for further spending and this can foster clear communication throughout the company.

- Budgets also help to get managers thinking more like accountants and really considering the financial realm. A good manager should be able to balance finances in their head but a well-structured budget will make the task even easier.

- There are different kinds of budgets such as master budgets, cash flow budgets, and operational budgets. Figuring out which type of budget your company should be using depends on the size, goals, and industry that the company exists within.

- Marginal analysis is an examination of the costs and benefits associated with any activity within the company. This is most often undertaken when considering how much product to produce or whether or not you should hire a new employee.

- Marginal analysis is the process through which we compare how much something costs to how much it is expected to help us. If we are increasing costs then we must also increase how much money we are making. Marginal analysis is one of the tools we use to achieve this.

- Marginal analysis believes that small changes have big effects. This means that a small change, such as hiring a new employee, has a big effect on how the future plays out. Marginal analysis basically estimates how the future would look if the company were to make one small change. This change is then calculated for and financial statements are generated to give an idea of how it will affect the company in the long run.

- Because marginal analysis is only focused on a single change at a time, you will find that you have to run several in order to weigh your options at any given time. If you have three options for how to act, marginal analysis must be run on each.

- When marginal analysis is run on one item, it may show that item would have a positive change on the company. Before you go ahead and implement that change, make sure to run marginal analysis on the other options. It could just be that another option has an even more positive effect.

- Cash flow analysis is the process of analyzing a cash flow statement. Cash flow statements show how much cash a company is dealing with but it merely serves as a snapshot of a moment in time. In order to truly benefit from this statement, you must perform analysis on it.

- Cash flow analysis is undertaken in order to see if you are making as much money as you should be. One of the biggest challenges that newer businesses face is to keep enough cash around to pay for the bills and keep the lights on. A cash flow statement shows you where your cash flow has been but a cash flow analysis is the process through which you read that data and come to an understanding of how it is functioning in the long term.

- Forecasting is the process through which accountants use data about the current and historical costs of production in order to predict the future cost. By using historical data an accountant is able to see how the price has changed between the historical figure and the current one. This change then lets the accountant forecast forward to predict how the price will continue to change in the future.

- Forecasting is not an exact science. Forecasting can never account for the weirdness of life like recessions or pandemics. Because of this it is important to keep in mind that a forecast is a prediction and not a guarantee. You can predict where the price will be but only time will tell you if that prediction was right or not.

- Forecasting can use the high-low method, in which the highest cost and highest cost-driver activity level is compared against the lowest cost and lowest level of cost-driver activity in order to make a prediction.

- Another approach is regression analysis which uses an independent and a dependent variable in order to forecast predictions.

- Financial leverage is using debt in order to purchase assets. Basically, it is using that new bank loan to purchase assets that will generate income for the company.

- Financial leverage can lead to enhanced earnings but it is also a riskier investment because you need to accrue debt to use. It isn't rare for a company to have too much financial leverage and be unable to pay the interest on it.

FINAL WORDS

There you have it: an introduction to accounting. I hope that this volume was able to give you a foundational education into the process of business accounting. There isn't enough space in one book to answer every possible question so I apologize if you have one left unanswered. Accounting is both a process in which we closely follow guidelines, either GAAP or IFRS, but there is a lot of room for variation. There is massive variation between companies that operate in vast and separate fields but even within a single industry there will be wildly different accounting needs that need to be handled.

The easiest need to understand is the need for financial reporting. No matter what field you are working in, your company must comply with the law and provide financial statements at regular intervals to stay on the right side of the law. Every single company has a need for financial accounting and it is this that we focused on the most throughout the book. This isn't the only type of accounting there is. In chapter one we looked at financial accounting and managerial accounting, our two big ones, but we also saw that there are other types of accounting such as tax accounting or forensic accounting. Another issue that we resolved was the confusion around bookkeeping and accounting. While both are important, and it makes sense for them to be linked together, they are still both different components of running a business. A lot of bookkeeping responsibilities have been taken over by accountants in the move to digital practices so it is common for accountants to need to learn the basics of bookkeeping these days.

In chapter two we looked at the basics of accounting. This chapter was used to define and explain some of the most important concepts in accounting. We looked at the accounting equation and saw it was made up of assets, liabilities, and shareholders' equity. To understand how these parts come together to fill out the accounting equation we looked at each of them up close to see what they mean, how they function, and how their importance is impossible to escape. Finally, we finished out this chapter with a look at what taxes are and what financial statements are. That wouldn't be the last time we explored financial statements though.

Before we could get back to financial statements we had to first learn about the various principles of accounting. We used chapter three for this purpose. We started by looking at five of the more important principles in the realm of accounting. These principles included concepts such as the full disclosure principle which reminds us to always fully disclose our earnings and the objectivity principle which reminds us that these statements are neutral and not meant to have our objective interpretation. These principles make for good accounting and they are important both for the Generally Accepted Accounting Principles (GAAP) and the International Financial Reporting Standards (IFRS). We saw that the GAAP is more rules-based while the IFRS is more standards-based. The GAAP is used in the USA while the rest of the world typically uses the IFRS. This chapter was closed out with a look at compliance and the eleven titles that were introduced in 2002 to make lack of compliance into more of a legal issue than it had been previously.

Chapter four saw us return to our financial statements. We started the chapter with a discussion of how to understand and best use financial statements. This included a discussion on their purpose, which is to say that they're used most frequently by investors, and this helped us to get a perspective on why they are so valuable. From there we moved into the financial statements themselves starting with the balance sheet, then the income statement, the cash flow statement, and finally the statement of retained earnings. These four financial statements are included together and generated for use outside of the company. Financial accounting is an external accounting system in this method.

In chapter five we had a discussion on bookkeeping. While bookkeeping is another discipline, it is a discipline that is being more and more wrapped into accounting every year. It would not surprise me if we saw bookkeeping as a field that shrinks dramatically going forward. In this chapter we looked at the purpose of a general ledger for keeping track of your financial transactions. How a general ledger works, how trial balance plays a role in the picture, and how we use debits, credits, and record journal entries were all covered so that you will have no problem using or reading a general ledger going forward.

Finally that brings us to chapter six where we turned our attention towards managerial accounting. This is the form of accounting that is focused on generating data and reports that managers and other higher-ups can use when deciding what steps the company should take next.

This included a discussion on why budgeting is so important, as well as discussions on how to perform marginal analysis, cash flow analysis, how to forecast into the future and how financial leverage works.

Together these chapters serve to give you a rough idea of the world of accounting. There is far more to it than what we've been able to cover today but our goal was never to become masters. I don't want to trick you into thinking that you're some kind of super accountant now. You're far from it. But you now have enough knowledge to generate, read, and analyze financial reports and ensure that your company's accounting never strays onto the wrong side of the law. If this book has given you any help in understanding your company then I will consider my job well done.

Don't forget that the learning doesn't have to stop here. There are lots of resources available for you to continue learning about and leveling up your accounting skills. For example, we've hardly even begun to touch on investment accounting or tax accounting. Now that you have the basics, you're better equipped to seeked out and understand whatever accounting questions you have next. Don't ever stop learning, it's the best way to continue improving your business.